The Child

Living to Please God and Your Parents

JOHN S.C. ABBOTT

SOLID GROUND CHRISTIAN BOOKS
Birmingham, Alabama USA

SOLID GROUND CHRISTIAN BOOKS
2090 Columbiana Rd., Suite 2000
Birmingham, AL 35216
(205) 443-0311
sgcb@charter.net
http://solid-ground-books.com

THE CHILD AT HOME:
Living to Please God and Your Parents

by John S.C. Abbott (1805-1877)

First published in 1833 by The American Tract Society, NY City, NY

SGCB Classic Reprints

ISBN: 1-932474-67-6

Cover Design by Borgo Design, Tuscaloosa, Alabama
Contact them by e-mail at nelbrown@comcast.net

Cover image from the oil painting entitled *The Destruction of 'L'Orient'
at the Battle of the Nile, August 1, 1798,* by George Arnald (1763-1841).
See *The Story of the Cover Image* following the Author's Preface.

Manufactured in the United States of America

The Author's Preface

This book is intended for the children of those families to which *The Mother at Home* has gone. It is prepared with the hope that it may exert an influence upon the minds of the children, in exciting gratitude for their parents' love, and in forming characters which shall ensure future usefulness and happiness.

The book is intended, not for entertainment, but for solid instruction. I have endeavored, however, to present instruction in an attractive form, but with what success, the result alone can tell. The object of the book will not be accomplished by a careless perusal. It should be read by the child, in the presence of the parent, that the parent may seize upon the incidents and remarks introduced, and thus deepen the impression made upon the child.

Though the book is particularly intended for children, or rather for young persons, it is hoped that it will aid parents in their efforts for moral and religious instruction.

It goes from the author with the most earnest prayer, that it may save some parents from blighted hopes, and that it may allure many children to gratitude, and obedience, and heaven.

John S.C. Abbott
Worcester, MA
December 1833

The Story of the Cover Image

The cover image was chosen for this book in honor of one of the heroes described in Chapter Three. *Casabianca* died on the ship pictured on the cover because he refused to abandon the sinking ship without the word of his father, the Captain of the vessel. You will read more of him in this precious book, but the story of the ship and its sinking is as follows:

When the government of revolutionary France received General Napoleon Bonaparte's proposal for an invasion of Egypt, they accepted with alacrity. If successful, the venture would threaten British interests in the Middle East and India. Whatever happened, it would send the ambitious and popular young Corsican on an expedition thousands of miles from Paris, from which he might never return.

Consequently, an army was embarked in Toulon and set sail for Malta on 19th May 1798. Landing virtually unopposed, they overthrew the moribund Knights of St John and established a French garrison in their place. Laden with loot from the Maltese churches and castles, they then set sail for Egypt. One foggy night they passed within a few miles of Nelson's pursuing British fleet, but managed to escape detection. On the night of 30th June the French army landed at Marabout Bay, 7 miles from Alexandria which they captured the next day. With barely a pause, Napoleon turned his attention to the interior and embarked on a grueling 19 day march southwards. After winning a spectacular battle in the shadow of the pyramids he captured Cairo and began to establish a government for Egypt.

Meanwhile the French fleet, under the command of Admiral Brueys, had moved along the coast to Aboukir Bay—Alexandria's harbor being too shallow to accommodate his warships. The fleet was in a bad way—under-manned and short of supplies—Brueys anchored his thirteen Ships of the Line along the western edge of the bay and sent many of his sailors ashore to find food and other supplies.

For all this time Rear Admiral Sir Horatio Nelson's British fleet had been cruising the Mediterranean seeking news of the French. They had already visited Alexandria once, leaving the city 25 hours before the French had arrived to search elsewhere, it wasn't until nearly a month after Napoleon's landing that they discovered their mistake. Reaching Alexandria on the 1st August they split up to find the enemy, locating Brueys' ships at 2:45. Brueys expected Nelson to gather his fleet for a battle the following day—as fighting amongst the shoals of the bay in failing light would be very risky. Nelson, who had already lost an eye and an arm in the service of his country, thrived on such risks—he directed his ships into the fray without delay.

The British fleet sailed steadily towards their opponents, led by the *Goliath*. When only 200 yards from the head of the French line, *Goliath's* captain, Thomas Foley, observed that they had anchored their ships just far enough into the bay to allow a ship to pass on the landward side. To the horror of his opponents, he steered his ship into this narrow channel, blasting the head of the French line as he did so. Four ships followed Foley, whilst the remainder tackled the seaward side with Nelson.

From this moment, the French fleet was doomed. Hemmed in by shallow water and adverse winds, they could not maneuver or bring most of their guns to bear on the enemy. The British were able to sail down the line picking off their opponents one by one. Some of the French ships had stores and provisions piled up against the gun-ports on their landward side—meaning they couldn't fire at *Goliath* and her followers at all, whilst under manning and lack of training weakened what firepower they were able to employ.

At the height of the action, a piece of shrapnel struck Nelson in the head. Stunned by the blow and believing himself to be mortally wounded, he was carried below by his men. The Admiral was not a man to pull rank in the station, and waited his turn to be treated. When the surgeon examined the wound he found it to be relatively minor—a deep gash had cut Nelson literally to the bone and caused a flap of skin to fall over his one good eye. Once bandaged up Nelson was able to stagger back on deck in time to see the climax of the action.

The pride of the French fleet, *l'Orient*, one of the biggest warships in the world, had caught fire and was burning out of control. As the flames began to engulf the French flagship, the 10-year old son of its commander, Captain Casabianca, was determined not to abandon his post without orders to do so from his father. The orders never came. The fire spread to the ship's magazine, causing a massive explosion that was heard 12 miles away in Alexandria. The youth and many of his shipmates perished in the blast. His devotion to duty was immortalized in Felicia Hemans' much parodied poem *Casabianca*:

> "The boy stood on the burning deck,
> Whence all but he had fled..."

The fighting carried on into the night and on into the next morning. In the end French fleet was almost totally destroyed, with only two of the original thirteen ships remaining. Napoleon was stranded in Egypt and, though he would win several dramatic victories on land, his weakness at sea doomed the Egyptian expedition to eventual failure. Nelson was made Baron Nelson of the Nile and Burnham Thorpe and sailed on to the adulation of his country and eventual apotheosis at Trafalgar seven years later.

Solid Ground Christian Books is delighted to introduce this reprint, *The Child at Home,* confident that it will be used to the eternal benefit of multitudes of children and parents.
Soli Deo Gloria!

The Publisher
January 2005

TABLE OF CONTENTS

CHAPTER ONE

RESPONSIBILITY—The Police Court. The widow and her daughter. Effect of a child's conduct upon the happiness of its parents. The young sailor. The condemned pirate visited by his parents. Consequences of disobedience. A mother's grave. The sick child...... 1

CHAPTER TWO

DECEPTION—George Washington and his hatchet.—Consequences of deception. Temptations to deceive. Story of the child sent on an errand. Detection. Anecdote. The dying child. Peace of a dying hour disturbed by falsehood previously uttered. Various ways of deceiving. Thoughts on death. Disclosures of the Judgment Day..................... 19

CHAPTER THREE

OBEDIENCE, I—Firmness requisite in doing duty. The irresolute boy. The girl and the green apples. Temptations. Evening party. Important consequences resulting from slight disobedience. The state prison. History of a young convict. Ingratitude of disobedience. The soldier's widow and her son. The Story of Casabianca. Cheerful obedience. Illustration. Parental kindness... 33

CHAPTER FOUR

OBEDIENCE, II —The moonlight game. Reasons why good parents will not allow their children to play in the streets in the evening. The evening walk. The terrified girl. Instance of filial affection. Anecdote. Strength of a mother's love. The child's entire dependence. A child rescued from danger. Child lost in the prairie...........................53

CHAPTER FIVE

RELIGIOUS TRUTH—Human character. The Northern Voyagers and their evil mutiny. Imaginary scene in a court of justice. Love of God. Scene from Shakespeare. Efforts to save us. The protection of angels. The evening party. The dissolute son. A child lost in the woods. The sufferings of the Savior. The Holy Spirit.. 71

CHAPTER SIX

PIETY—Penitence. George Jones. His idleness. Charles Bullard. His good character in school. In college. The pious boy. The orchard. The fishing-rod. The forgiving spirit. How children may do good. The English clergyman and the child who gave himself to the Savior. The happy sick boy. The Christian child in heaven. Uncertainty of life. The loaded gun. The boy in the stage-coach.. 91

CHAPTER SEVEN

TRAITS OF CHARACTER—We cannot be happy without friends. Why students are unpopular in school. The way to gain friends. The warm fire. Playing ball. Recipe for children who would be loved. A bad temper. Amiable disposition to be cultivated. The angry man. Humility. The vain young lady. Vanity always ridiculous. The affected school girl. The unaffected school-girl. Story of the proud girl. Moral courage. The duelist. The three school-boys. George persuaded to throw the snow-ball. What would have been real moral courage. The boy leaving home. His mother's provisions for his comfort. The parting. His father's memorable counsel. His reflections in the stage-coach. He consecrates himself to his Maker............... 113

"Honour thy father and thy mother:
that thy days may be long upon the land
which the LORD thy God giveth thee."
Exodus 20:12

"Ye shall fear every man his mother, and his father,
and keep my sabbaths: I am the LORD your God."
Leviticus 19:3

"Honour thy father and thy mother,
as the LORD thy God hath commanded thee;
that thy days may be prolonged,
and that it may go well with thee,
in the land which the LORD thy God giveth thee."
Deuteronomy 5:16

"Children, obey your parents in the Lord:
for this is right.
Honour thy father and mother;
(which is the first commandment with promise;)
That it may be well with thee,
and thou mayest live long on the earth."
Ephesians 6:1-3

Chapter One

Responsibility

In large cities there are so many persons guilty of crimes, that it is necessary to have a court sit every day to try those who are accused of breaking the laws. This court is called the Police Court. If you should go into the room where it is held, you would see the officers bringing in one after another of miserable and wicked creatures, and, after stating and proving their crimes, the judge would command them to be led away to prison. They would look so wretched that you would be shocked in seeing them.

One morning a poor woman came into the Police Court in Boston. Her eyes were red with weeping, and she seemed to be borne down with sorrow. Behind her followed two men, leading in her daughter.

"Here, sir," said a man to the judge "is a girl who behaves so badly that her mother cannot live with her, and she must be sent to the House of Correction."[1]

"My good woman," said the judge, "what is it that your daughter does which renders it so uncomfortable to live with her?"

---

[1] House of Correction - (formerly) a jail or other place of detention for persons convicted of minor offences.

"Oh, sir," she replied, "it is hard for a mother to accuse her own daughter, and to be the means of sending her to the prison. But she behaves so as to destroy all the peace of my life. She has such a temper, that she sometimes threatens to kill me, and does every thing to make my life wretched."

The unhappy woman could say no more. Her heart seemed bursting with grief, and she wept aloud. The heart of the judge was moved with pity, and the bystanders could hardly refrain from weeping with this afflicted mother. But there stood the hard-hearted girl, unmoved. She looked upon the sorrows of her mother in sullen silence. She was so hardened in sin, that she seemed perfectly insensible to pity or affection. And yet she was miserable. Her countenance showed that passion and malignity filled her heart, and that the fear of the prison, to which she knew she must go, filled her with rage.

The judge turned from the afflicted mother, whose sobs filled the room, and, asking a few questions of the witnesses, who testified to the daughter's ingratitude and cruelty, ordered her to be led away to the House of Correction. The officers of justice took her by the arm, and carried her to her gloomy cell. Her lonely and sorrowing mother went weeping home to her abode of poverty and desolation. Her own daughter was the viper which had stung her bosom. Her own child was the wretch who was filling her heart with sorrow.

And while I now write, this guilty daughter is occupying the gloomy cell of the prison, and this widowed mother is in her silent dwelling, in loneliness and grief! Oh, could the child who reads these pages, see that mother and that daughter now, you might form some feeble idea of the consequences of disobedience; you might see how unutterable the sorrow a wicked child may bring upon herself and upon her parents. It is not easy, in this case, to judge which is the most unhappy, the mother or the child. The mother is broken-hearted at home. She is alone and friendless. All her hopes are most cruelly destroyed. She loved her daughter, and hoped that she would live to be her friend and comfort. But instead of that, she became her curse, and is bringing her mother's gray hairs in sorrow to the grave.[2] And then look at the daughter—guilty and abandoned—Oh, who can tell how miserable she must be!

Such is the grief which children may bring upon themselves and their parents. You probably have never thought of this very much. *I write this book that you may think of it, and that you may, by obedience and affection, make your parents happy, and be happy yourselves.*

This wicked girl was once a playful child, innocent and happy. Her mother looked upon her with most ardent love, and hoped that her dear daughter would live to be her companion and friend. At first she ventured to disobey in some trifling thing. She still loved her mother, and would have been struck with horror at the thought of being guilty of crimes which she afterwards committed. But she went on from bad to worse, every day growing more disobedient, until she made her poor mother so miserable that she almost wished to die, and till she became so miserable herself, that life must have been a burden. You think, perhaps, that you never shall be so unkind and wicked as she finally became. But if you begin as she began, by trifling disobedience, and little acts of unkindness, you may soon be as wicked as she, and make your parents as unhappy as her poor broken-hearted mother.

---

[2] This expression is found in Genesis 42:38; 44:29,31.

Persons never become so very wicked all at once. They go on from step to step, in disobedience and ingratitude, till they lose all feeling, and can see their parents weep, and even die in their grief, without a tear.

Perhaps, one pleasant day, this mother sent her little daughter to school. She took her books, and walked along, admiring the beautiful sunshine, and the green and pleasant fields. She stopped one moment to pick a flower, again to chase a butterfly, and again to listen to a little robin, pouring out its clear notes upon the branch of some lofty tree. It seemed so pleasant to be playing in the fields that she was unwilling to go promptly to school. She thought it would not be *very wrong* to play a *little while.* Thus she commenced. The next day she ventured to chase the butterflies farther, and to rove more extensively through the field in search of flowers. And as she played by the pebbles in the clear brook of rippling water, she forgot how fast time was passing. And when she afterwards hastened to school, and was asked why she was so late, to conceal her fault she was guilty of falsehood, and said that her mother wanted her at home. Thus she advanced rapidly in crime. Her lessons were neglected. She loved the fields better than her books, and would often spend the whole morning idle, under the shade of some tree, when her mother thought her safe in school. Having thus become a truant and a deceiver, she was prepared for any crimes. Good children would not associate with her, and consequently she had to choose the worst for her companions and her friends. She learned wicked language; she was rude and vulgar in her manners; she indulged ungovernable passion; and at last grew so bad, that when her family afterwards moved to the city, the House of Correction became her shameful home. And there she is now, guilty and wretched. And her poor mother, in her solitary dwelling, is weeping over her daughter's disgrace. Who can comfort such a mother? Where is there any earthly joy to which she can look?

Children generally do not think how much the happiness of their parents depends upon their conduct. But you now see how very unhappy you can make them. And is there a child who reads this book, who would be willing to be the cause of sorrow to his father and his mother? After all they have done for you, in taking care of you when an infant, in watching over you when sick, in giving you clothes to wear, and food to eat, can you be so ungrateful as to make them unhappy? You have all read the story of the kind man, who found a viper lying upon the ground almost dead with cold. He took it up and placed it in his bosom to warm it, and to save its life. And what did that viper do? He killed his benefactor! Vile, vile reptile! Yes! As soon as he was warm and well, he stung the bosom of his kind preserver, and killed him.

But that child is a worse viper, who, by his ingratitude, will sting the bosoms of his parents; who, by disobedience and unkindness, will destroy their peace, and thus dreadfully repay them for all their love and care. God will not forget the sins of such a child. His eye will follow you to see your sin, and his arm will reach you to punish. He has said, "Honor your father and your mother."[3] And the child who does not do this, must meet with the displeasure of God, and must be for ever shut out from heaven. Oh, how miserable must this wicked girl now be, locked up in the gloomy prison! But how much more miserable will she be when God calls her to account for all her sins!—when, in the presence of all the angels, the whole of her conduct is brought to light, and God says to

---

[3] Exodus 20:12; Deuteronomy 5:16; Malachi 1:6; Matthew 15:4,6; 19:19; Mark 7:10; 10:19; Luke 18:20; Ephesians 6:2

her, "Depart from me, ye cursed!"[4] As she goes away from the presence of the Lord, to the gloomy prisons of eternal despair, she will then feel a degree of remorse which I cannot describe to you. It is painful to think of it. Ah, wretched, wretched girl! Little are you aware of the woes you are preparing for yourself. I hope that no child who reads these pages will ever feel these woes.

You have just read that it is in your power to make your parents very unhappy; and you have seen how unhappy one wicked girl made her poor mother. I might tell you many such melancholy stories, all of which would be true. A few years ago there was a boy who began to be disobedient to his parents in little things. But every day he grew worse, more disobedient and willful, and troublesome. He would run away from school, and thus grew up in ignorance. He associated with bad boys, and learned to swear and to lie, and to steal. He became so bad that his parents could do nothing with him. Every body who knew him, said, "That boy is preparing for the gallows."[5] He was the pest of the neighborhood. At last he ran away from home, without letting his parents know that he was going. He had heard of the sea, and thought it would be a very pleasant thing to be a sailor. But nothing is pleasant to the wicked. When he came to the seashore, where there were a large number of ships, it was some time before any one would hire him, because he knew nothing about a ship or the sea. There was no one there who was his friend, or who pitied him, and he sat down and cried bitterly, wishing he was at home again, but ashamed to go back. At last a sea captain came along, and hired him to go on a distant voyage; and as he knew

---

[4] Matthew 7:23; 25:41; Luke 13:27.
[5] The gallows was an instrument of punishment whereon criminals were executed by hanging.

nothing about the rigging of a vessel, he was ordered to do the most servile work on board. He swept the decks and the cabin, and helped the cook, and was the servant of all. He had the poorest food to eat he ever ate in his life. And when night came, and he was so tired that he could hardly stand, he had no soft bed upon which to lie, but could only wrap a blanket around him, and throw himself down any where to get a little sleep. This unhappy boy had acquired so sour a disposition, and was so disobliging, that all the sailors disliked him, and would do every thing they could to tease him. When there was a storm, and he was pale with fear, and the vessel was rocking in the wind, and pitching[6] over the waves, they would make him climb the mast, and laugh to see how terrified he was, as the mast reeled to and fro, and the wind almost blew him into the raging ocean. Often did this poor boy get into some obscure part of the ship, and weep as he thought of the home he had forsaken. He thought of his father and mother, how kind they had been to him, and how unkind and ungrateful he had been to them, and how unhappy he had made them by his misconduct. But these feelings soon wore away. Familiarity with sea life gave him courage, and he became calloused to its hardships. Constant intercourse with the most profligate and abandoned, gave strength and inveteracy[7] to his sinful habits; and before the voyage had terminated, he was reckless of danger, and as hardened and unfeeling as the most depraved on board the ship. This boy commenced with disobedience in little things, and grew worse and worse, till he forsook his father and his mother, and was prepared for the

---

[6] In navigation, pitching is the rising and falling of the head and the stern of the ship.

[7] Inveteracy is firmness or deep-rooted obstinacy of any quality or state acquired by time.

abandonment of every virtue, and the commission of any crime. But the eye of God was upon him, following him wherever he went, and marking all his iniquities. An hour of retribution was approaching. It is not necessary for me to trace out to you his continued steps of progress in sin. When on shore, he passed his time in haunts of dissipation. And several years rolled on in this way, he growing more hardened, and his aged parents, in their loneliness, weeping over the ruin of their guilty and wandering son.

One day an armed vessel sailed into one of the principal ports of the United States, accompanied by another, which had been captured. When they arrived at the wharf, it was found that the vessel taken was a pirate. Multitudes flocked down upon the wharf to see the pirates as they were led off to the prison, there to await their trial. Soon they were brought out of the ship, with their hands fastened with chains, and led through the streets. Ashamed to meet the looks of honest men, and terrified with the certainty of condemnation and execution, they walked along with downcast eyes and trembling limbs. Among the number was seen the unhappy and guilty boy, now grown to be a young man, whose history we are relating. He was locked up in the dismal dungeon of a prison. The day of trial came. Pale and trembling, he was brought before the judge. He was clearly proved guilty, and sentenced to be hung. Again he was carried back to his prison, there to remain till the hour for his execution should arrive. News was sent to his already broken-hearted parents that their son had been condemned as a pirate, and was soon to be hung. The news was almost too much for them to endure. In an agony of feeling which cannot be described, they wept together. They thought of the hours of their child's infancy, when they watched over him in sickness, and soothed him to sleep. They thought how happy they felt when they saw the innocent smile play upon his childish cheek. They thought of the joy they then anticipated in his opening years, and of the comfort they hoped he would be to them in their declining days. And now to think of him, a hardened criminal, in the murderer's cell!—Oh, it was too much, too much for them to bear. It seemed as though their hearts would burst. Little did they think, when, with so much affection they caressed their infant child, that he would be the curse of their life, embittering all their days, and bringing down their gray hairs with sorrow to the grave. Little did they think that his first trifling acts of disobedience would lead on to such a career of misery and of crime. But the son was sentenced to die, and the penalty of the law could not be avoided. His remorse and his parents' tears could be of no avail. Agonizing as it would be to their feelings, they felt that they must go and see their son before he should die.

One morning, a gray-headed man, and an aged and sickly woman, were seen walking along, with faltering footsteps, through the street which led to the prison. It was the heart-broken father and mother of this unnatural child. When they came in sight of the gloomy granite walls and iron-grated windows of this dreary abode, they could hardly proceed, so overwhelming were the feelings which pressed upon their minds. When arrived at the door of the prison, the aged father, supporting upon his arm the weeping and almost fainting mother, told the jailer who they were, and requested permission to see their son. Even the jailer, accustomed as he was to scenes of suffering, could not witness this exhibition of parental grief without being moved to tears. He led the parents through the stone galleries of the prison, till they came to the iron door of the cell in which their son was confined. As he turned the key with all his strength, the heavy bolt flew back, and he opened the door of the cell. Oh, what a sight for a father and a mother to gaze upon! There was just enough light in this gloomy abode to show them their son, sitting in the corner on the stone floor, pale and emaciated, and loaded with chains. The moment the father beheld the pale features of his long-absent son, he raised his hands in the agony of his feelings, and fell fainting at his feet. The mother burst into loud exclamations of grief, as she clasped her son, guilty and wretched as he was, to her maternal bosom. Oh, who can describe this scene! Who can conceive the anguish which wrung the hearts of these afflicted parents! And it was their own boy, whom they had loved and cherished, who had brought all this woe upon them. I cannot describe to you the scene which ensued. Even the very jailer could not bear it, and he wept aloud. At last he was compelled to tear the parents away; and it was agonizing indeed to leave their son in such a situation, soon to be led to a shameful death. They would gladly have stayed and died with their guilty child. But it was necessary that they should depart; and, the jailer having closed the door and turned the massive bolt, they left the unhappy criminal in his cell. Oh, what would he have given, again to be innocent and free! The parents returned to their home, to weep by day and by night, and to have the image of their guilty son disturbing every moment of peace, and preventing the possibility of joy. The day of execution soon arrived, and their son was led to the gallows, and launched into eternity. And, crimsoned with guilt, he went to the bar of God,[8] there to answer for all the crimes of which he had been guilty, and for all the woes he had caused.

---

[8] The bar of God is the final tribunal where we will give an account to God on the Day of Judgment (cf. Romans 14:10-12; 2 Cor. 5:10).

You see, then, how great are your responsibilities as a child. You have thought, perhaps, that you have no power over your parents, and that you are not accountable for the sorrow which your conduct may cause them. Do you think that God will hold this child guiltless for all the sorrow he caused his father and his mother? And do you think God will hold any child guiltless, who shall, by his misconduct, make his parents unhappy? No. You must answer to God for every thing you do, which gives your parents pain. And there is no sin greater in the sight of God than that of an ungrateful child. I have shown you, in the two illustrations which you have just read, how much the happiness of your parents depends upon your conduct. Every day you are promoting their joy or their sorrow. And every act of disobedience, or of ingratitude, however trifling it may appear to you, is, in the eyes of your Maker, a sin which cannot pass unnoticed. Do you ask, 'Why does God consider the ingratitude of children as a sin of peculiar aggravation?' I reply, 'Because you are under peculiar obligation to love and obey your parents. They have loved you when you could not love them. They have taken care of you when you could not reward them. They have passed sleepless nights in listening to your cries, and weary days in watching over you, when you could neither express thanks nor feel grateful. And after they have done all this, is it a small sin for you to disobey them and make them unhappy?'

And indeed you can do nothing to make *yourself* so unhappy as to indulge in disobedience, and to cherish a spirit of ingratitude. You never see such a child happy. Look at him at home, and, instead of being light-hearted and cheerful, he is sullen and morose. He sits down by the fireside in a winter evening, but the evening fireside affords no joy to him. He knows that his parents are grieved at his conduct. He loves nobody, and feels that nobody loves him. There he sits silent and sad, making himself miserable by his own misconduct. The disobedient boy or girl is always unhappy. You know how different the dispositions of children are. Some are always pleasant and obliging, and you love their company. They seem happy when they are with you, and they make you happy. Now you will almost always find that such children are obedient to their parents. They are happy at home, as well as abroad. God has in almost every case connected enjoyment with duty, and sorrow with sin. But in no case is this connection more intimate, than in the duty which children owe their parents.

And to every child who reads this book, I would say, *If you wish to be happy, you must be good.* Do remember this. Let no temptation induce you for a moment to disobey. The more ardently you love your parents, the more ardently will they love you. But if you are ungrateful and disobedient, childhood will pass away in sorrow; all who are virtuous will dislike you, and you will have no friends worth possessing. When you arrive at mature age, and enter upon the active duty of life, you will have acquired those feelings which will deprive you of the affection of your fellow beings, and you will probably go through the world unloved and unrespected. Can you be willing so to live?

The following account, written by one who, many years after her mother's death, visited her grave, forcibly describes the feelings which the remembrance of the most trifling act of ingratitude will, under such circumstances, awaken.

"It was thirteen years since my mother's death, when, after a long absence from my native village, I stood beside the sacred mound, beneath which I had seen her buried. Since that mournful period, a great change had come over me. My childish years had passed away, and with them my youthful character. The world was altered too; and as I stood at my mother's grave, I could hardly realize, that I was the same thoughtless, happy creature, whose cheeks she so often kissed in an excess of tenderness. But the varied events of thirteen years had not effaced the remembrance of that mother's smile. It seemed as if I had seen her but yesterday—as the blessed sound of her well-remembered voice was in my ear. The happy dreams of my infancy and childhood were brought back so distinctly to my mind, that, had it not been for one bitter recollection, the tears I shed would have been gentle and refreshing. The circumstance may seem a trifling one, but the thought of it now pains my heart, and I relate it, that those children who have parents to love them may learn to value them as they ought.

"My mother had been ill a long time, and I became so accustomed to her pale face and weak voice, that I was not frightened at them, as children usually are. At first, it is true, I sobbed violently; but when, day after day, I returned from school, and found her the same, I began to believe she would always be spared to me. But they told me she would die.

"One day, when I had lost my place in the class, and had done my work incorrectly, I came home discouraged and fretful. I went to my mother's chamber. She was paler than usual, but she met me with the same affectionate smile that always welcomed my return. Alas, when I look back through the lapse of thirteen years, I think my heart must have been stone not to have melted by it. She requested me to go down stairs and bring her a glass of water. I irritably asked why she did not call a domestic to do it. With a look of mild reproach, which I shall never forget, if I live to be a hundred years old, she said, 'And will not my daughter bring a glass of water for her poor sick mother?'

"I went and brought her the water, but I did not do it kindly. Instead of smiling and kissing her, as I was wont to do, I set the glass down very quickly, and left the room. After playing about a short time, I went to bed without bidding my mother good night. But when alone in my room, in darkness and in silence, I remembered how pale she looked, and how her voice trembled when she said, 'Will not my daughter bring a glass of water for her poor sick mother?' I could not sleep. I slipped into her bed chamber to ask forgiveness. She had sunk into an easy slumber, and they told me I must not waken her. I did not tell any one what troubled me, but slipped back to my bed, resolved to rise early in the morning, and tell her how sorry I was for my conduct.

"The sun was shining brightly when I awoke; and, hurrying on my clothes, I hastened to my mother's chamber. She was dead! She never spoke more—never smiled upon me again—and when I touched the hand that used to rest upon my head in blessing, it was so cold that it made me jump. I bowed down by her side, and sobbed in the bitterness of my heart. I thought then I might wish to die, and be buried with her, and, old as I now am, I would give worlds, were they mine to give, could my mother but have lived to tell me that she forgave my childish ingratitude. But I cannot call her back; and when I stand by her grave, and whenever I think of her manifold kindness, the memory of that reproachful look she gave me will bite like a serpent and sting like an adder."

And when your mother dies, do you not think that you will feel remorse for every unkind word you have uttered, and for every act of ingratitude? Your beloved parents must soon die. You will probably be led into their darkened chamber, to see them pale and helpless on their dying bed. Oh, how will you feel in that solemn hour! All your past life will come to your mind, and you will think that you would give worlds, if you could blot out the remembrance of past ingratitude. You will think that, if your father or mother should only get well, you would never do any thing to grieve them again. But the hour for them to die must come. You may weep as though your heart would break, but it will not recall the past, and it will not delay their death. They must die; and you will probably gaze upon their cold and lifeless countenances in the coffin. You will follow them to the grave, and see them buried for ever from your sight. Oh, how unhappy you will feel, if you then have to reflect upon your misconduct! The tears you will shed over their graves will be the bitterer, because you will feel that, perhaps, your own misconduct hastened their death.

But perhaps you will die before your parents do. If you go into the grave-yard, you will see the graves of many children. You know that the young are liable to die, as well as the old. And what must be the feelings of the dying child, who knows that he is going to appear before God in judgment, and yet feels conscious that he has been unkind to his parents! Oh, such a child must fear to go into the presence of his Maker. He must know that God will never receive into heaven children who have been so wicked. I have seen many children die. And I have seen some, who had been very amiable and pleasant all their lives, when they came to die, feel grieved that they had not been more careful to make their parents happy. I knew one affectionate little girl, who was loved by all who knew her. She hardly ever did any thing which was displeasing to her parents. But one day she was taken sick. The doctor was called; but she grew worse and worse. Her parents watched over her with anxiety and tears, but still her fever raged, and death drew nearer. At last all hopes of her recovery were over, and it was known that she must die. Then did this little girl, when she felt that she must leave her parents for ever, mourn that she had ever done any thing to give them pain. The most trifling act of disobedience, and the least unkindness of which she had ever been guilty, then came fresh into her mind, and she could not die in peace, till she had called her father and her mother to her bedside, and implored their forgiveness. If so obliging and affectionate a little girl as this felt so deeply in view of the past, when called upon to die, how agonizing must be the feelings which will crowd upon the heart of the wicked and disobedient child who has filled her parents' heart with sorrow!

But you must also remember that there is a Day of Judgment to come. You must appear before God to answer for every thing you have done or thought while in this world. Oh, how will the ungrateful child then feel! Heaven will be before him, in all its beauty and bliss, but he cannot enter.

"Those holy gates for ever bar
Pollution, sin and shame."

He has, by his ingratitude, made a home on earth unhappy, and God will not permit him to destroy the happiness of the homes in heaven.

He will see all the angels in their holiness and their joy, but he cannot be permitted to join that blessed throng. With his ungrateful heart he would but destroy their enjoyment. The frown of God must be upon him, and he must depart to that wretched world where all the wicked are assembled. There he must live in sorrows which have

16

no end. *Oh, children, how great are your responsibilities!* The happiness of your parents depends upon your conduct. And your ingratitude may fill your lives with sorrow, and your eternity with woe. Will you not, then, read this book with care, and pray that God will aid you to obey its directions, that your homes on earth may be joyful, and that you may be prepared for happier homes beyond the stars?

Chapter Two

Deception

Probably nearly all who read this book have heard the story of George Washington and his hatchet. George, when a little boy, had received from his father a hatchet, and he, much pleased with his present, walked around the yard trying its keen edge upon every thing which came within his reach. At last he came to a favorite pear-tree of his father's, and began, with great dexterity, to try his skill in felling trees. After hacking upon the bark until he had completely ruined the tree, he became tired, and went into the house. Before long, his father, passing by, beheld his beautiful tree entirely ruined; and, entering the house, he earnestly asked who had been guilty of the destruction. For a moment George trembled and hesitated. He was strongly tempted to deny that he knew any thing about it. But summoning all his courage, he replied, "Father, I cannot tell a lie. I cut it with my hatchet." His father clasped him to his arms, and said, "My dear boy, I would rather lose a thousand trees than have my son a liar."

This little anecdote shows that George Washington, when a boy, was too brave and noble to tell a lie. He had rather be punished than be so wretched and degraded as to utter a falsehood. He did wrong to cut the pear-tree, though, perhaps, he did not know the extent of the injury he was doing. But had he denied that he did it, he would have been a cowardly and disgraceful liar. His father would have been ashamed of him, and would never have known when to believe him. If little George Washington had told a lie then, it is by no means improbable that he would have gone on from falsehood to falsehood, till every body would have despised him. And he would thus have become a disgrace to his parents and friends, instead of a blessing to his country and the world. No boy, who has one particle of that noble spirit which George Washington had, will tell a lie. It is one of the most degrading of sins. There is no one who does not regard a liar with contempt. Almost always, when a lie is told, two sins are committed. The first is, the child has done something which he knows to be wrong. And the second is, that he has not courage enough to admit it, and tells a lie to hide his fault. And therefore, when a child tells a lie, you may always know that that child is a coward. George Washington was a brave man. When duty called him, he feared not to meet danger and death. He would march to the mouth of the cannon in the hour of battle; he would ride through the field when bullets were flying in every direction, and strewing the ground with the dead, and not a nerve would tremble. Now, we see that George Washington was brave when a boy, as well as when a man. He scorned to tell a lie, and, like a noble-hearted boy, as he was, he honestly avowed the truth. Every body admires courage, and every body despises cowardice. The liar, whether he be a boy or a man, is looked upon with disgust.

Cases will occur in which you will be strongly tempted to say that which is false. But if you yield to the temptation, how can you help despising yourself? A little girl once came into the house and told her mother something which was very improbable. Those who were sitting in the room with her mother did not believe her, for they did not know the character of the little girl. But the mother replied at once, "I have no doubt that it is true, for I never knew my daughter to tell a lie." Is there not something noble in having such a character as this? Must not that little girl have felt happy in the consciousness of thus possessing her mother's entire confidence? Oh, how different must have been her feelings from those of the child whose word cannot be believed, and who is regarded by every one with suspicion! Shame, shame on the child who has not magnanimity[9] enough to tell the truth.

God will not allow such sins to go unpunished. Even in this world the consequences are generally felt. God has given every person a conscience, which approves that which is right, and condemns that which is wrong. When we do any thing wrong, our consciences punish us for it, and we are unhappy. When we do any thing that is right, the approval of conscience is a reward. Every day you feel the power of this conscience approving or condemning what you do. Sometimes a person thinks that if he does wrong, and it is not found out, he will escape punishment. But it is not so. He will be punished whether it is found out or not. Conscience will punish him if no one else does.

There was once a boy whose father sent him to ride a few miles upon an errand, and told him particularly not to stop by the way. It was a beautiful and sunny morning in the spring; and as he rode along by the green fields, and heard the singing of the birds as they flew from tree to tree, he felt as light-hearted and as happy as they. After

---

[9] Magnanimity – Greatness of mind; that elevation or dignity of soul, which encounters danger and trouble with tranquility and firmness.

doing his errand, however, as he was returning by the house where two of his friends and playmates lived, he thought he could not resist the temptation just to call a moment to see them. He thought there would be no great harm if he merely stopped a minute or two, and his parents would never know it. Here commenced his sin. He stopped, and was led to remain longer and longer, till he found he had passed two hours in play. Then, with a troubled conscience, he mounted his horse, and set his face towards home. The fields looked as green and the skies as bright and cloudless, as when he rode along in the morning; but, oh, how different were his feelings! Then he was innocent and happy; now he was guilty and wretched. He tried to feel easy, but he could not; conscience reproached him with his sin. He rode sadly along, thinking what excuse he should make to his parents for his long absence, when he saw his father, at a distance, coming to meet him. His father, fearing that some accident had happened, left home in search of his son. The boy trembled and turned pale as he saw him approaching, and hesitated whether he had better confess the truth at once, and ask forgiveness, or endeavor to hide the crime with a lie. Oh, how much better it would have been for him if he had acknowledged the truth! How much sooner would he have been restored to peace! But one sin almost always leads to another. When this kind father met his son with a smile, the boy said, "Father, I lost the road, and it took me some time to get back again, and that is the reason why I have been gone so long."

His father had never known him to be guilty of falsehood before, and was so happy to find his son safe, that he did not doubt what he said was true. But, oh, how guilty, and ashamed, and wretched, did that boy feel, as he rode along! His peace of mind was destroyed. A heavy weight of conscious guilt pressed upon his heart. The boy went home and repeated the lie to his mother. It is always thus when we turn from the path of duty; we know not how widely we shall wander. Having committed one fault, he told a lie to conceal it, and then added sin to sin, by repeating and persisting in his falsehood. What a change had one short half day produced in the character and the happiness of this child! His parent had not yet detected him in his sin, but he was not, on that account, free from punishment. Conscience was at work, telling him that he was degraded and guilty. His look of innocence and his lightness of heart had left him. He was ashamed to look his father or mother in the face. He tried to appear easy and happy, but he was uneasy and miserable. A heavy load of conscious guilt rested upon him, which destroyed all his peace.

When he retired to bed that night, he feared the dark. It was long before he could quiet his troubled spirit with sleep. And when he awoke in the morning, the consciousness of his guilt had not forsaken him. There it remained fixed deep in his heart, and would allow him no peace. He was guilty, and of course wretched. The first thought which occurred to him, on waking, was the lie of the preceding day. He could not forget it. He was afraid to go into the room where his parents were, lest they should discover, by his appearance, that he had been doing something wrong. And though, as weeks passed away, the acuteness of his feelings in some degree abated, he was all the time disquieted and unhappy. He was continually fearing that something would occur which should lead to his detection.

Thus things went on for several weeks, till, one day, the gentleman at whose house he stopped called at his father's on business. As soon as this boy saw him come into the house, his heart beat violently, and he turned pale with the fear that something would be said that would bring the whole truth to light. The gentleman, after conversing a few moments with his father, turned to the little boy, and said, "Well, how did you get home the other day? My boys had a very pleasant visit from you." Can you imagine how the boy felt? You could almost have heard his heart beat. The blood rushed into his face, and he could not speak; and he dared not raise his eyes from the floor. The gentleman then turned to his parents, and said, "You must let your son come up again and see my boys. They were quite disappointed when he was there a few weeks ago, for he only stayed about two hours, and they hoped he had come to spend the whole day with them." There, the whole truth was out. And how do you suppose that boy felt? He had disobeyed his parents; told a lie to conceal it; had for weeks suffered the pangs of a guilty conscience; and now the whole truth was discovered. He stood before his parents overwhelmed with shame, convicted of disobedience, and wretched, degraded falsehood.

This boy was all the time suffering the conesquences of his sin. For many days he was enduring the reproaches of conscience, when the knowledge of his crime was confined to his own bosom. How bitterly did he suffer for the few moments of forbidden pleasure he had enjoyed! The way of the transgressor is always hard.[10] Every child who does wrong must, to a greater or less degree, feel the same sorrows. This guilty child, overwhelmed with confusion and disgrace, burst into tears, and implored his parents' forgiveness. But he was told by his parents that he had sinned, not only against them, but against God. The humble child went to God in penitence and in prayer. He made a full confession of all

---

[10] Proverbs 13:15.

to his parents, and obtained their forgiveness; and it was not till then that peace of mind was restored.

Will not the child who reads this account take warning from it? If you have done wrong, you had better confess it at once. Falsehood will but increase your sin, and aggravate your sorrow. Whenever you are tempted to say that which is untrue, look forward to the consequences. Think how much sorrow, and shame, and sin, you will bring upon yourself. Think of the reproaches of conscience; for you may depend upon it, that those reproaches are not easily borne.

And is it pleasant to have the reputation of a liar? When persons are detected in one falsehood, they cannot be believed when they speak the truth. No person can place any more confidence in them till a long time of penitence has elapsed, in which they have had an opportunity to manifest their amendment. The little boy, whose case we have above alluded to, was sincerely penitent for his sin. He resolved that he never would tell another lie. But since he had deceived his parents once, their confidence in him was necessarily for a time destroyed. They could judge of the reality of his penitence only by his future conduct. One day he was sent to a store to purchase some small articles for his mother. In his haste, he forgot to stop for the few cents of change which he ought to have received. Upon his return home, his mother inquired for the change. He had not thought a word about it before, and very frankly told her, that he had forgotten it entirely. How did his mother know that he was telling the truth? She had just detected him in one lie, and feared that he was now telling her another. "I hope, my dear son," she said, "you are not again deceiving me." The boy was perfectly honest this time, and his parents had never before distrusted his word. It almost broke his heart to be thus suspected, but he felt that it was just, and went to his chamber and wept bitterly. These are the necessary consequences of falsehood. A liar can never be believed. It matters not whether he tells truth or falsehood; no one can trust his word. If you are ever tempted to tell a lie, first ask yourself whether you are willing to have it said that nobody can trust your word. The liar is always known to be such. A person may possibly tell a lie which shall not be detected, but almost always something happens which brings it to light. The boy, who stopped to play when on an errand two miles from his father's house, thought that his falsehood would never be discovered. But he was detected, and overwhelmed with shame.

It is impossible for a person who is in the habit of uttering untruths to escape detection. Your character for truth or falsehood will be known. And what can be more humiliating and degrading than to have the name of a liar? It is so considered in all nations and with all people. It is considered one of the vilest and most cowardly vices of which one can be guilty. The liar is always a coward. He tells lies, because he is afraid to tell the truth.

And how do you suppose the liar must feel when he comes to die? It is a solemn hour. Perhaps many of the children who read this book have never seen a person die. I have seen many. I have seen children of all ages dressed in the shroud and placed in the coffin. I might write pages in describing to you such scenes. One day, I went to see a little girl about ten years of age, who was very sick. When I went into the room, she was lying upon the little cot-bed, her lips parched with fever, and her face pale and emaciated with suffering. Her mother was standing by her bedside, weeping as though her heart would break. Other friends were standing around, looking in vain for something to do to relieve the little sufferer. I went and took her by the hand, and found that she was dying. She raised her languid eyes to me, but could not speak. Her breathing grew fainter and fainter. Her arms and limbs grew cold. We could only look mournfully on and see the advances of death, without being able to do any thing to stop its progress. At last she ceased to breathe. Her spirit ascended to God to be judged, and her body remained upon the bed, a cold and lifeless corpse. All children are exposed to death; and when you least expect it, you may be called to lie upon a bed of sickness, and go down to the grave. There is nothing to give one joy in such an hour, but a belief that our sins are forgiven, and that we are going to the heavenly home. But how must a child feel in such an hour, when reflecting upon falsehoods which are recorded in God's book of remembrance! Death is terrible to the impenitent sinner; but it is a messenger of love and of mercy to those who are prepared to die. If you have been guilty of a falsehood, you cannot die in peace till you have repented and obtained forgiveness.

There was a little girl eleven years of age, who died a few months ago. She loved the Savior, and when told that she would not live, was very happy. She said she was happy to die, and go home and be with her Savior and the angels in heaven. But there was one thing, which, for a time, weighed heavily upon her mind. A year or two before she felt interested in religion she had told a lie to her aunt; and she could not die in peace, till she had seen that aunt, confessed her sin, and asked forgiveness. Her aunt was sent for, though she was many miles distant. When her aunt came, the sick little girl, with sorrow for her fault, made confession, and asked forgiveness, "Aunt," said she, "I have prayed to God, and hope that he has forgiven me; and I cannot die in peace till I have obtained your forgiveness." If any child who reads this book is tempted to deceive his parents or his friends, I hope he will remember that he must soon die, and think how he will feel in that solemn hour.

But perhaps you think that the falsehood of which this girl was guilty was one of peculiar aggravation. It was simply this: She was one day playing in the room with several little children, and was making them laugh very loud. Her aunt said, "My dear, you must not make them laugh so loud."

And she replied, "It is not I, aunt, who makes them laugh."

This was the falsehood she uttered. And though her aunt did not know that it was false, the little girl did, and God in heaven did. And when she came to die, though it was a year or two after, her soul was troubled, and the consciousness of her sin destroyed her peace. A lie is, in the sight of God, a dreadful sin, be it ever so trifling in our estimation. When we are just ready to leave the world, and to appear before God in judgment, the convictions of a guilty conscience will press upon the heart like lead.

There are many ways of being guilty of falsehood without uttering the lie direct in words. Whenever you try to deceive your parents, in doing that which you know they disapprove, you do, in reality, tell a lie. Conscience reproves you for falsehood. Once, when I was in company, as the plate of cake was passed round, a little boy, who sat by the side of his mother, took a much larger piece than he knew she would allow him to have. She happened, for the moment, to be looking away, and he broke a small piece off and covered the rest in his lap with his handkerchief. When his mother looked, she saw the small piece, and supposed he had taken no more. He intended to deceive her. His mother has never found out what he did. But God saw him, and frowned upon him, as he committed this sin.

And do you not think that the boy has already suffered for it? Must he not feel wretched and contemptible whenever he thinks that, merely to get a little bit of cake, he would deceive his kind mother? If that little boy had one particle of honorable or generous feeling remaining in his bosom, he would feel reproached and unhappy whenever he thought of his wretchedness. If he was already dead to shame, it would show that he had by previous deceit acquired this character. And can any one love or esteem a child who has become so degraded? And can a child, who is neither beloved nor respected, be happy? No! You may depend upon it, that when you see a person guilty of such deceit, he does in some way or other, even in this world, suffer a severe penalty. A frank and open-hearted child is the only happy child. Deception, however skillfully it may be practiced, is disgraceful, and ensures sorrow and contempt. If you would have the approbation of your own conscience, and the approval of friends, never do that which you shall desire to have concealed. Always be open as the day. Be above deceit, and then you will have nothing to fear. There is something delightful in the magnanimity of a perfectly sincere and honest child. No person can look upon such a one without affection. You are sure of friends, and your prospects of earthly usefulness and happiness are bright.

But we must not forget that there is a day of most solemn judgment near at hand. When you die, your body will be wrapped in the shroud, and placed in the coffin, and buried in the grave; and there it will remain and decompose to the dust, while the snows of unnumbered winters, and the tempests of unnumbered summers, shall rest upon the cold earth which covers you. But your spirit will not be there. Far away, beyond the cloudless skies, and blazing suns, and twinkling stars, it will have gone to judgment. How awful must be the scene which will open before you, as you enter the eternal world! You will see the throne of God: how bright, how glorious, will it burst upon your sight! You will see God the Savior seated upon that majestic throne. Angels, in numbers more than can be counted, will fill the universe with their glittering wings, and their rapturous songs. Oh, what a scene to behold! And then you will stand in the presence of this countless throng to answer for every thing you have done while you lived. Every action and every thought of your life will then be fresh in your mind. You know it is written in the Bible, "God will bring every work into judgment, with every secret thing, whether it be good or whether it be evil."[11] How must the child then feel who has been guilty of falsehood and deception, and has it then all brought to light! No liar can enter the kingdom of heaven. Oh, how dreadful must be the confusion and shame with which the deceitful child will then be overwhelmed! The angels will all see your sin and your disgrace. And do you think they will wish to have a liar enter heaven, to be associated with them? No! They must turn from you with disgust. The Savior will look upon you in his displeasure. Conscience will rend your soul. And you must hear the awful sentence, "Depart from me, into everlasting fire, prepared for the devil and his angels."[12] Oh, it is a dreadful thing to practice deceit. It will shut you from heaven. It will confine you in eternal woe. Though you should escape detection as long as you live; though you should die, and your falsehood not be discovered, the time will soon come when it will all be brought to light, and when the whole universe of men and of angels will be witnesses of your shame. If any child who reads this feels condemned for

---

[11] Ecclesiastes 12:14.
[12] Matthew 25:41.

past deception, oh, beware, and do not postpone repentance till the Day of Judgment shall arrive. Go at once to those whom you have deceived, and make confession, and implore forgiveness. Then go to your Savior, fall upon your knees before him; pray that he will pardon you, and promise to sin no more. If your prayer is offered in sincerity, and your resolution remains unbroken, the Savior will forgive you; and when the trump of the archangel shall summon you to judgment, he will give you a home in heaven. The tear of sincere penitence our kind Savior is ever ready to accept.

If you are ever tempted to deceive, O, remember, that your deception must soon be known. It is utterly impossible that it should long remain undetected. The moment the Day of Judgment arrives, your heart will be open to the view of the universe, and every thought will be publicly known. How much safer then is it to be sincere and honest! Strive to preserve your heart free from guile. Then you will have peace of conscience. You will fear no detection. You can lie down at night in peace. You can awake in the morning with joy. Trusting in the Savior for acceptance, you can die happy. And when the morning of the resurrection dawns upon you, your heart will be filled with a joy which earth's sunniest mornings and brightest skies never could afford. The Savior will smile upon you. Angels will welcome you to heaven. You will rove, in inexpressible delight, through the green pastures of that blissful abode. You will lie down by the still waters where there is sweet repose for ever. Oh, what an hour of bliss must that be, when the child, saved from sin and sorrow,

"Has reached the shore
Where tempests never beat nor billows roar!"

Chapter Three

Obedience - Part I

In the chapters you have now read, I have endeavored to show you how much your own happiness, and that of your parents, depends upon your conduct. And I trust every child who has read thus far, has resolved to do all in his power to promote the happiness of those who have been so kind to him. But you will find that it is a very different thing to resolve to do your duty, from what it is to perform your resolutions when the hour of temptation comes. It requires courage and firmness to do right, when you are surrounded by those who urge you to do wrong. Temptations to do wrong will be continually arising; and, unless you have resolution to brave ridicule, and to refuse solicitation, you will be continually led into trouble. I knew a young man who was ruined entirely, because he had not courage enough to say no. He was, when a boy, very amiable in his disposition, and did not wish to make any person unhappy; but he had no mind of his own, and could be led about by his associates into almost any difficulties, or any sins. If, in a clear moonlight winter evening, his father told him he might go out doors, and slide down the hill for half an hour, he would resolve to be obedient and return home at the time appointed. But if there were other boys there, who should tease him to remain longer; he had not the courage to refuse. And thus he would disobey his kind parents because he had not courage to do his duty. He began in this way, and so he continued. One day, a bad boy asked him to go into a store, and drink some brandy. He knew it was wrong, and did not wish to go. But he feared that, if he did not, he would be laughed at; and so he went. Having thus yielded to this temptation, he was less prepared for temptation again. He went to the bottle with one and another, till at last he became intemperate, and would stagger through the streets. He fell into the company of gamblers, because he could not refuse their solicitations. He thus became a gambler himself, and went on from step to step, never having resolution to say no, till he ruined himself, and planted within him the seeds of disease, which hurried him to a premature grave. He died the miserable victim of his own irresolution.

Thousands have been thus ruined. They are amiable in disposition, and in general mean well, but have not courage to do their duty. They fear that others will laugh at them. Now, unless you are sufficiently brave not to care if others do laugh at you; unless you have sufficient courage to say no, when others tempt you to do wrong, you will be always in difficulty: such a person never can be happy or respected. You must not expect it will be always easy to do your duty. At times it will require a great mental struggle, and call into exercise all the resolution you possess. It is best that it should be so, that you may acquire firmness of character and strength of integrity. Near a schoolhouse in the country, there was an apple-tree. One summer it was covered with hard, and sour, and green apples, and the little girls who went to that school could hardly resist the temptation of eating those apples, though they knew there was danger of its making them sick. One girl, who went to that school, was expressly forbidden by her mother from eating them. But when all her playmates were around her, with the apples in their hands, and urging her to eat, telling her that her mother never would know it, she wickedly yielded to their solicitation. She felt guilty, as, in disobedience to her mother's commands, she ate the forbidden fruit. But she tried to appease her conscience by thinking that it would do no harm. Having thus commenced disobedience, she would every day eat more freely, and with less reluctance. At last she was taken sick. Her mother asked her if she had been eating any of the green apples at school. Here came another temptation to sin. When we once commence doing wrong, it is impossible to tell where we shall stop. She was afraid to acknowledge to her mother her disobedience; and to hide the fault she told a lie. She declared that she had not eaten any of the apples. Unhappy girl! She had first disobeyed her mother, and then told a lie to conceal her sin. But she continually grew sicker, and it became necessary to send for the physician. He came, and when he had looked upon her feverish countenance, and felt her throbbing pulse, he said there was something upon her stomach which must be removed. As he was preparing the nauseous emetic, the conscience-smitten girl trembled for fear that her disobedience and her falsehood should both be brought to light. As soon as the emetic operated, her mother saw, in the *half-chewed fragments of green apples,* the cause of her sickness. What could the unhappy and guilty girl say? Denial was now, of course, out of the question. She could only cover her face with her hands, in the vain attempt to hide her shame. We hope that this detection and mortification will teach that little girl a lesson which she will never forget. And we hope that the relation of the story will induce every child, who reads it, to guard against temptation, and boldly to resist every allurement to sin.

Temptations will be continually coming, which you will find it hard to resist. But if you once yield, you have entered that downward path which leads inevitably to sorrow and shame. How much wiser would it have been in the little girl, whose story we have just related, if she had in the first instance resolutely refused to disobey her mother's command! How much happier would she have been, when retiring to sleep at night, if she had the joy of an approving conscience, and could, with a grateful heart, ask the blessing of God! The only path of safety and happiness is implicit obedience. If you, in the slightest particular, yield to temptation, and do that which you know to be wrong, you will not know when or where to stop. To hide one crime, you will be guilty of another; and thus you will draw down upon yourself the frown of your Maker, and expose yourself to sorrow for time and eternity.

And think not that these temptations to do wrong will be few or feeble. Hardly a day will pass in which you will not be tempted, either through indolence to neglect your duty, or to do that which you know your parents will disapprove. A few years ago, two little boys went to pass the afternoon and evening at the house of one of their playmates, who had a party, to celebrate his birthday. Their parents told them to come home at eight o'clock in the evening. It was a beautiful afternoon, late in the autumn, as the large party of boys assembled at the house of their friend. Numerous barns and sheds were attached to the house, and a beautiful grove of beech and of oak trees surrounded it, affording a most delightful place for all kinds of sport. Never did boys have a more happy time.

They climbed the tree, and swung upon the limbs. And as they jumped upon the new-made hay in the barns, they made the walls ring with their joyous shouts. Happiness seemed, for the time, to fill every heart. They continued their sports till the sun had gone down behind the hills, and the last ray of twilight had disappeared. When it became too dark for outdoor play, they went into the house, and commenced new games in the brightly-lighted parlor. As they were in the midst of the exciting game of "blind man's bluff," some one entered the room, and requested them all to take their seats, for apples and nuts were to be brought in. Just as the door was opened by the servant bringing in the waiter loaded with apples and nuts, the clock struck eight. The boys, who had been told to leave at that hour, felt troubled enough. They knew not what to do. The temptation to stay was almost too strong to be resisted. The older brother of the two faintly whispered to one at his side, that he must go. Immediately there was an uproar all over the room, each one exclaiming against it.

"Why," said one, "my mother told me I might stay till nine."

"My mother," said another, "did not say any thing about my coming home: she will let me stay as long as I want to."

"I would not be tied to my mother's apron-string," said a rude boy, in a distant part of the room.

A timid boy, who lived in the next house to the one in which these two little boys lived, came up, and said, with a very imploring countenance and voice, "I am going home at half past eight. Now do stay a little while longer, and then we will go home together. I would not go alone, it is so dark."

And even the lady of the house where they were visiting, came to them and said, "I do not think your mother will have any objection to have you stay a few moments longer, and eat an apple and a few nuts. I would have sent them in earlier, if I had known that you wanted to go."

Now, what could these poor boys do? How could they summon resolution to resist so much entreaty? For a moment they hesitated, and almost yielded to the temptation. But virtue wavered only for a moment. They immediately mustered all their courage, and said, "We must go." Hastily bidding them all good night, they got their hats as quick as they could, for fear, if they delayed, they should yield to the temptation, and left the house. They stopped not a moment to look back upon the brightly-shining windows, and happy group of boys within, but, taking hold of each other's hands, ran as fast as they could on their way home. When they arrived at home, their father and mother met them with a smile. And when their parents learnt under what strong temptations they had been to disobey, and that they had triumphed over these temptations, they looked upon their children with feelings of gratification, which amply repaid them for all their trial. And when these boys went to bed that night, they felt that they had done their duty, and that they had given their parents pleasure; and these thoughts gave them vastly more happiness than they could have enjoyed if they had remained with their playmates beyond the hour which their parents had permitted. This was a noble proof of their determination to do their duty. And, considering their youth and inexperience, and the circumstances of the temptation, it was one of the severest trials to which they could be exposed. Probably, in all their after life, they would not be under stronger temptations to swerve from duty. Now, every child will often be exposed to similar temptations. And if your resolution be not strong, you will yield. And if you once begin to yield, you will never know where to stop but, in all probability, will go on from step to step till you are for ever lost to virtue and to happiness.

But perhaps some child, who reads this, thinks I make too serious a matter of so slight a thing. You say, It cannot make *much difference* whether I come home half an hour earlier or later. But you are mistaken here. It does make a great difference. Think you God can look upon the disobedience of a child as a trifling sin? Is it a trifle to refuse to obey parents who have loved you, and watched over you for months and for years; who have taken care of you in sickness, and endeavored to relieve you when in pain; who have given you clothes to wear, and food to eat, and have done all in their power to make you happy? It is inexcusable ingratitude. It is awful sin. But perhaps you ask, What positive harm does it do? It teaches your parents that their child is unwilling to obey them; and is there no harm in that? It makes your parents unhappy; and is there no harm in that? It tempts you to disobey in other things; and is there no harm in that? It is entering upon that career of sin which led the girl, whom we have, in the first chapter, described to you, to the house of correction, and the wretched boy to the gallows. Oh, beware how you think it is a little thing to disobey your parents! Their happiness is in a great degree in your hands; and every thing which you knowingly do that disturbs their happiness in the least degree is sin in the sight of God; and you must answer for it at his bar.

If you go into any state prison, you will see a large number of men working in silence and in gloom. They are dressed in clothes of contrasted colors, that, in case of escape, they may be easily detected. But the constant presence of vigilant keepers, and the high walls of stone, guarded by an armed sentry, render escape almost impossible. There many of these guilty men remain, month after month, and year after year, in friendlessness, and in silence, and in sorrow. They are in confinement and disgrace. At night, they are marched to their solitary cells, there to pass the weary hours, with no friend to converse with, and no joy to cheer them. They are left, in darkness and in solitude, to their own gloomy reflections. And, oh! how many bitter tears must be shed in the midnight darkness of those cells! How many an unhappy criminal would give worlds, if he had them to give, that he might again be innocent and free! You will see in the prison many who are young—almost children. If you go around from cell to cell, and inquire how these wretched persons commenced their course of sin, very many will tell you that it was with disobedience to parents. You will find prisoners there, whose parents are most affectionate and kind. They have endeavored to make their children virtuous and happy. But, oh! how cruelly have their hopes been blasted! A disobedient son has gone from step to step in crime, till he has brought himself to the gloomy cell of the prison, and has broken his parents' hearts by his disobedience.

The chaplain of the Massachusetts state prison recently communicated to the public the following interesting narrative of the progress of crime.

"A few weeks ago, I addressed the congregation to which I minister, on the importance of a strict attention to what are usually denominated *little things;* and remarked, that it is the want of attention to these *little things,* which not unfrequently throws a disastrous influence over the whole course of subsequent life. It was also further remarked, that a large proportion of the events and transactions, which go to make up the lives of most men, are, as they are usually estimated, comparatively unimportant and trivial; and yet, that all these events and transactions contribute, in a greater or less degree, to the formation of character; and that on *moral character* are suspended, essentially, our usefulness and happiness in time, and our well-being in eternity.

"I then remarked, that I could not doubt, but, on sober reflection, many of that assembly would find that they owed the complexion of a great portion of their lives, and their unhappy situation as tenants of the state prison, to some event or transaction comparatively trivial, and of which, at the time, they thought very little. I requested them to make the examination, and see whether the remark I had made was not correct.

"This was on the Sabbath. The next morning, one of the prisoners, an interesting young man, came to me, and observed, that he should be glad to have some conversation with me, whenever I should find it convenient. Accordingly, in the afternoon of the same day, I sent for him. On his being seated, and my requesting him to state freely what he wished to say, he remarked, 'that he wished to let me know how peculiarly appropriate to his case were the observations I had made, the previous day, on the influence of little things; and if I would permit him, he would give me a brief sketch of his history; and, particularly, of the transaction, which, almost in childhood, had given a disastrous coloring to the whole period of his youth, and, in the result, had brought him to be an occupant of his present dreary abode.'

"It appears, from the sketch which he gave, that he was about ten years of age, when his father moved from a distant part of the state to a town in the vicinity of Boston. In this town was a respectable boarding-school, not a great

41

distance from the residence of his father; and to this school he was sent. Having always lived in the country, he had seen very few of those novelties, and parades, and shows, which are so common in and near the city; and it is not strange, that, when they occurred, he should, like most children, feel a strong desire to witness them.

"Before he had been long at school, he heard there was to be a *"Cattle Show"* at Brighton. He had never seen a *Cattle Show*. He presumed it must be a very interesting spectacle, and felt a very strong desire to attend. This desire, on the morning of the first day of the show, he expressed to his father, and was told that it would be a very improper place for him to go to, unless attended by some suitable person to watch over and take care of him; and that such was the business of the father, that he could not accompany him, and, of course, his desire could not be gratified. He was sorely disappointed, but resolved not to give up, without further effort, an object on which his heart was so much set.

"The next morning he entreated his father again on the subject. His father seemed anxious to have his son gratified, but told him that he could by no means consent to have him go to such a place without suitable company; and, though his business was urgent, he would try to go in the afternoon; and, if he did, he would call at the school-house, and take him with him. This was all he could promise.

"But here was an *uncertainty*, an *if*, which very illy accorded with the eager curiosity of the son. Accordingly, he resolved that he would go at all hazards. He doubted much whether his father would go, and if he *did not*, he concluded he might, without much difficulty, conceal the matter from him. Having formed his determination and laid his plan, he went, before leaving home in the morning, to his father's desk, and took a little money to spend on the occasion; and, instead of going to school, went to Brighton. Contrary, however, to his expectations and hopes, his father, for the sake of gratifying him, concluded to go to the show, and, on his way, called for him at school. But no son was to be found, and no son had been there that day. The father, during the afternoon, saw the son, but took care that the son should not discover him. After the return of both at evening, the father inquired of the son whether he had attended school that day. His reply was that he had. My youthful readers will perceive how readily and naturally one fault leads to another. But the son was soon satisfied from further questions, and from the manner of his father, that he knew where he had been; and he confessed the whole.

"The father told him that he should feel himself bound in duty to acquaint his teacher with the affair, and to request him to call him to account for absenting himself thus from the school without permission, and to inflict such punishment on him as might be thought proper.

"He was, accordingly, sent to school, and, in his view, disgraced in the estimation of his teacher and of his school-fellows; and he resolved not to submit to it for any great length of time. A few days after this, he left home, under pretence of going to school, and ran away. He traveled on, until he reached the town from which his father had removed, and had been absent for several weeks before his parents ascertained what had become of him. He was, however, discovered, and brought back to his home.

"Some time after this, he was sent to another school, in a neighboring town; but, not being altogether pleased, he resolved, as he had run away once, he would try the experiment again; and this he did. He had been

THE CHILD AT HOME

absent six months before his parents ascertained what had become of him. He had changed his name; but, getting into some difficulty, in consequence of which he must go to jail, unless he could find friends, he was constrained to tell his name, and who were his parents; and in this way his good father, whom he had so much abused, learning his son's condition, stepped in to his aid, and saved him from confinement in a prison.

"But I should make this story much too long, were I to detail all the particulars of his subsequent life until he became a tenant of the state prison. Suffice it to say, that he went on from one mis-step to another, until he entered upon that career of crime which terminated as before stated.

"And now, beloved reader, to what do you think this unhappy young man ascribes his wanderings from home, and virtue, and happiness, and the forlorn condition in which he now finds himself? Why, simply, to the *trivial circumstance* of his leaving school one day, without his father's consent, for the purpose of going to a cattle show! And what do you think he says of it now? 'I feel,' said he, 'that all I have suffered, and still suffer, is the righteous chastisement of heaven. I deserve it all, for my wicked disobedience both to my earthly and my heavenly Father; and I wish,' said he, further, 'that you would make such use of my case as you shall think best calculated to instruct and benefit the young.'

"And now, beloved reader, I have drawn up this sketch—and I can assure you it is no fictitious one—for your perusal. You here see what has been the result of a single act of disobedience to a parent; what it has already cost this unhappy man to gratify, in an unlawful way, his youthful curiosity even in a single instance.

"May He, who giveth wisdom to all who ask it, lead and guide you safely through the journey of life, and cause that even this humble sketch shall serve to strengthen you in virtue, and to deter you from the paths of the Destroyer."

Can any child read this narrative without trembling at the thought of disobedience, even in the most trifling affair? If you once disobey your parents, it is impossible to tell to what it will lead. Crime follows in the steps of crime, till the career is closed by irretrievable disgrace and eternal ruin. The consequences reach far, far beyond the grave. They affect our interests and our happiness in that eternal world to which we are all rapidly going. Yes; the child who utters one falsehood, or is guilty of one act of disobedience, may, in consequence of that one yielding to temptation, be hurried on from crime to crime, till his soul is ruined, and he is shut up, by the command of God, in those awful dungeons of endless despair prepared for the devil and his angels.

And how ungrateful is disobedience! A noble-hearted boy would deny himself almost any pleasure; he would meet almost any danger; he would endure almost any suffering, before he would, in the most trifling particular, disobey parents who had been so kind, and had endured so much to make him happy. How different is such a child from one who is so ungrateful that he will disobey his parents merely that he may play a few moments longer, or that he may avoid some trifling work, that he does not wish to perform! There is a magnanimity in a child who feels so grateful for his parents' love that he will repay them by all the affection and obedience in his power, which attracts the respect and affection of all who know him.

Suppose you see a little boy walking before his mother. The boy's father is dead; he has been killed in battle. You see the orphan boy carrying upon his shoulder his father's sword and cap. You look at his poor mother. She is weeping, for her husband is dead. She is returning in sorrow to her lonely house. She has no friend but her dear boy. How ardently does she love him! All her hopes of earthly happiness are depending upon his obedience and affection. She loves her boy so well, that she would be willing to die, to make him happy. She will work night and day, while he is young, to supply him with clothes and with food. And all she asks and hopes is that her boy will be affectionate, and obedient, and good.

And, oh! how ungrateful and cruel will he be, if he neglect that mother, and by his unkindness cause her to weep! But you see that he looks like a noble-hearted boy. His countenance seems to say, "Dear mother, do not cry; if ever I grow up to be a man, you shall never want, if I can help it." Oh, who can help loving the boy who loves his mother!

There was a little boy about thirteen years old, whose name was Casabianca. His father was the commander of a ship of war called the Orient. The little boy accompanied his father to the seas. His ship was once engaged in a terrible battle upon the river Nile. In the midst of the thunders of the battle, while the shots were flying thickly around, and strewing the decks with blood, this brave boy stood by the side of his father, faithfully discharging the duties which were assigned to him. At last his father placed him in a particular part of the ship, to be performing some service, and told him to remain in his post till he should call him away. As the father went to some distant part of the ship to notice the progress of the battle, a ball from the enemy's vessel laid him dead upon the deck. But the son, unconscious of his father's death, and faithful to the trust reposed in him, remained in his post, waiting for his father's orders. The battle raged dreadfully around him. The blood of the slain flowed at his feet. The ship took fire, and the threatening flames drew nearer and nearer. Still this noble-hearted boy would not disobey his father. In the face of blood, and balls, and fire, he stood firm and *obedient*. The sailors began to desert the burning and sinking ship, and the boy cried out "Father, may I go?" But no voice of permission could come from the mangled body of his lifeless father. And the boy, not knowing that he was dead, would rather die than disobey. And there that boy stood, at his post, till every man had deserted the ship; and he stood and perished in the flames. O, what a boy was that! Every body who ever heard of him thinks that he was one of the noblest boys that ever was born. Rather than disobey his father, he would die in the flames. This account has been written in poetry, and, as the children who read this book, may like to see it, I will present it to them here:—

CASABIANCA

The boy stood on the burning deck,
  Whence all but him had fled;
The flame that lit the battle's wreck,
  Shone round him o'er the dead.

Yet beautiful and bright he stood,
  As born to rule the storm;
A creature of heroic blood,
  A proud, though childlike form.

The flames rolled on; he would not go,
  Without his father's word;
That father, faint in death below,
  His voice no longer heard.

He called aloud—"Say, father, say
  If yet my task is done."
He knew not that the chieftain lay
  Unconscious of his son.

"Speak, father," once again he cried,
  "If I may yet be gone."
And—but the booming shots replied,
  And fast the flames rolled on.

Upon his brow he felt their breath,
  And in his waving hair;
And looked from that lone post of death,
  In still, yet brave despair;

And shouted but once more aloud,
  "My father, must I stay?"
While o'er him fast, through sail and shroud,
  The wreathing fires made way.

They wrapped the ship in splendor wild,
  They caught the flag on high,
And streamed above the gallant child,
  Like banners in the sky.

Then came a burst of thunder sound—
  The boy—oh! where was he?
Ask of the winds that far around
  With fragments strewed the sea.

With mast, and helm, and pennon fair,
That well had borne their part,
But the noblest thing that perished there,
Was that young, faithful heart.[13]

O, who would not love to have such a child as that! Is not such a boy nobler than one who will disobey his parents merely that he may have a little play, or that he may avoid some unpleasant duty? The brave little Casabianca would rather die than disobey. He loved his father. He had confidence in him. And even when death was staring him in the face, when

"The flames rolled on, he would not go,
Without his father's word."

I have seen some bad boys who thought it looked brave to care nothing for the wishes of their parents. But do you think that Casabianca was a coward? No; the boy who is truly brave, and has a noble spirit, will obey his parents. If others tease him to do differently, he will dare to tell them that he means to do his duty; and if they laugh at him, he will let them laugh, and show them, by his conduct, that he does not care for the sneers of bad boys. The fact is, that, in almost all cases, disobedient boys are wretched, and cowardly, and contemptible. They have not one particle of the spirit of the noble little Casabianca. And when these disobedient boys grow up to be men, they do not command influence or respect.

If you would be useful and happy when you arrive at mature years, you must be affectionate and obedient as a child. It is invariably true that the path of duty is the path

---

[13] Written by Felicia Dorthea Hemans (1793-1835) from her volume *The Poetical Works of Felicia Dorthea Hemans.*

of peace. The child who has established principles of firm integrity—who has that undaunted resolution which can face opposition and brave ridicule—bids fair to rise to eminence in usefulness and respect. These qualities, which shed so lovely a charm over childhood, will go with you into more mature life; they will give stability to your character, and command respect. And those faults of childhood which render one hesitating, and weak, and cowardly, will, in all probability, continue through your whole earthly existence. The man is but the grown-up child, possessing generally the same traits of character in every period of life. How important it is then that, in early youth, you should acquire the habit of triumphing over temptation, and of resolutely discharging all your duties!

It is important for you to remember that obedience requires of you, not only to do as you are bidden, *but to do it with cheerfulness and alacrity.* Suppose, as you are sitting at the table in a pleasant evening, the customary hour for you to retire to rest arrives. You are, perhaps, engaged in reading some very interesting book, and do not feel at all sleepy. You ask permission to sit up a little longer. But your mother tells you that the time for you to go to bed has come, and she prefers that you should be regular in your habits. You think it is rather severe that you cannot be indulged in your wishes, and, with sullen looks, shut your book, and, taking a light, in ill humor go to your chamber. Now, this is not obedience. As you retire to your chamber, the displeasure of God follows you. Your sin of disobedience is so great, that you cannot even pray before you fall asleep. It is impossible for a person to pray when out of humor. You may repeat the words of prayer, but you cannot offer acceptable prayer to the Lord. And as you lie down upon your bed, and the darkness of night is around you, your offended Maker regards you as an ungrateful and disobedient child. And all the night long his eye is upon your heart, and the knowledge of your sin is in his mind. Obedience belongs to the heart, as well as to the outward conduct. It is necessary that you should, with affection and cheerfulness, fulfill the wishes of your parents. You should feel that they know what is best, and, instead of being sullen and displeased because they do not think fit to indulge you in all your wishes, you should, with a pleasant countenance and a willing heart, yield to their requirements.

You do not know how much pleasure it affords your parents to see you happy. They are willing to make almost any sacrifice for your good. And they never have more heartfelt enjoyment themselves than when they see their children virtuous, contented, and happy. When they refuse to gratify any of your desires, it is not because they do not wish to see you happy, but because they see that your happiness will be best promoted by refusing your request. They have lived longer in the world than you, and know better than you the dangers by which you are surrounded. Deeply interested in your book, you desire to sit up later than usual, and think it would make you happy. But your mother, who is older and wiser, knows that the way to make children healthy and happy is to have them in the regular habit of retiring early at night. And when you ask to sit up later than usual, she loves you too well to permit it. You think she is cruel, when, in fact, she is as kind as she can be. If she were an unkind mother, and cared nothing about your happiness, she would say, "O yes; you may sit up as long as you please. I do not care any thing about it."

Now, is it obedience, when your kind mother is doing all in her power to make you happy, for you to look sullen and morose? Is it honoring your father and your mother, for you to look offended and speak unkindly, because they wish you to do that which they know to be for your welfare? The truly grateful child will endeavor, always, with a pleasant countenance, and a peaceful heart, to yield ready obedience to his parents' wishes. He will never murmur or complain. Such a child can retire to bed at night contented and happy. He can sincerely thank God for all his goodness and pray for that protection which God is ever ready to grant those who love him.

Chapter Four

Obedience - Part II

There is hardly any subject upon which children in well-regulated families feel more like complaining, than of the unwillingness of their parents to indulge them in evening games and evening visits. An active boy, whose heart is full of fun and frolic, is sitting quietly by the fireside, in a pleasant winter evening. Every now and then he hears the loud shouts and joyful laughter of some twenty of his companions, who are making the moonlight air ring with their merriment. Occasionally, a troop of them will go rushing by the windows, in the impetuosity of their sports. The ardent little fellow by the fireside can hardly contain himself. He longs to unite his voice in the shouts, and try his feet in the chase. He nestles upon his chair, and walks across the room, and peeps through the curtains. As he sees the dark forms of the boys clustered together in merry groups, or scattered in their games, he feels as though he were a prisoner. And even though he be a good boy, and obedient to his parents, he can hardly understand why it is that they deprive him of this pleasure. I used to feel so when I was a boy, and I suppose other boys feel the same. But now I see the reason. Those night games led the boys into bad habits. All kinds of boys met together, and some

53

would use indecent and profane language, which depraved the hearts and corrupted the morals of the rest. The boys, who were thus spending their evenings, were mis-improving their time, and acquiring a distaste for the purifying and peaceful enjoyments of home. You sometimes see men who appear to care nothing about their families. They spend their evenings away from home with the idle and the dissolute. Such men are miserable and despised. Their families are forsaken and unhappy. Why do these men do so? Because, when they were boys, they likely spent their evenings away from home, playing in the streets. Thus home lost all its charms, virtue was banished from their bosoms, and life was robbed of its joy. I wish every boy who reads this would think of these reasons, and see if they are not sufficient. Your kind parents do not allow you to go out in the evenings and play in the streets—

I. Because you will acquire bad habits. You will grow rude and vulgar in manners, and acquire a relish for pleasures which will destroy your usefulness and your happiness.

II. You will always find in such scenes bad boys, and must hear much indecent and profane language, which will corrupt your heart.

III. You will lose all fondness for the enjoyment of home, and will be in great danger of growing up a dissipated and a worthless man.

Now, are not these reasons sufficient to induce your parents to guard you against such temptations? But perhaps you say, '*Other parents* let *their* children go out and play as much as they please every evening.' How grateful, then, ought you to be, that you have parents who are so kind and faithful that they will preserve you from these occasions of sin and sorrow! They love you too well to be willing to see you preparing for an unhappy and profitless life.

It not infrequently is the case that a girl has young associates, who are in the habit of walking without protectors in the evening twilight. On the evening of some lovely summer's day, as the whole western sky is blazing with the golden hue of sunset, her companions call at her door, to invite her to accompany them upon an excursion of pleasure. She runs to her parents with her heart bounding with joy, in anticipation of the walk. They inquire into the plans of the party, and find that it will be impossible for them to return from their contemplated expedition before the darkness of the evening shall come. As affectionate and faithful parents, they feel that it is not proper or safe for them to trust their little daughter in such a situation. They, consequently, cannot consent that she should go. She is disappointed in the extreme, and as she sees her friends departing, social and happy, she retires to her chamber and weeps. The momentary disappointment to her is one of the severest she can experience, and she can hardly help feeling that her parents are cruel; to deprive her of so much anticipated pleasure. Her companions go away with the same feelings. They make many severe remarks, and really think that this little girl's parents are unkind. Perhaps they have a pleasant walk, and all return home in safety; and for many days they talk together at school of the delightful enjoyments of that evening. And this increases the impression on the mind of the little girl that it was unkind in her parents not to let her go.

But, perhaps, as they were returning, they met a drunken man, who staggered in amongst them. Terrified, they scatter and run. One, in endeavoring to jump over a fence, spoils her gown. Another, fleeing in the dark, falls, and sadly bruises her face. Another, with loss of bonnet, and with disheveled hair, gains the door of her home. And thus is this party, commenced with high expectations of joy, terminated with fright and tears. The parents of the little girl, who remained at home, knew that they were exposed to all this; and they loved their daughter too well to allow her to be placed in such a situation. Was it not kindness in them that led to their decision?

Perhaps, as they were returning, they met some twenty or more of the rudest boys of the village, in the midst of their most exciting sports. Here are Emma, Maria, and Susan, with their party of timid girls, who must force their way through this crowd of turbulent and noisy boys. It is already dark. Some of the most unmannerly and wicked boys of the village are there assembled. They are highly excited with their sports. And the moment they catch a view of the party of girls, they raise a shout, and rush in among them reckless and thoughtless. The parents of the little girl, who stayed at home, knew that she would be exposed to such scenes; and as they loved their daughter, they could not consent that she should go. Was it not kind?

A few young girls once went on such an evening walk, intending to return before it was dark. But in the height of their enjoyment they forgot how rapidly the time was passing, and twilight leaving them. But, at last, when they found how far they were from home, and how dark it was growing, they became quite alarmed, and hastened homeward. They, however, got along very well while they were all together. But when it became necessary for them to separate, to go to their respective homes, and several of them had to go alone in the darkness, they felt quite terrified. It was necessary for one of these little girls, after she had left all her companions, to go nearly a quarter of a mile. She set out upon the run, her heart beating with fear.

She had not proceeded far, however, before she heard the loud shouts of a mob of young men and boys, directly in the street through which she must pass. As she drew nearer, the shouts and laughter grew louder and more appalling. She hesitated. But what could she do? She must go on. Trembling, she endeavored to glide through the crowd, when a great brutal boy, with a horrid mask on his face and a "jack-o'lantern" in his hand, came up before her. He threw the glare of the light upon her countenance, and stared her full in the face. "Here is my wife," said he, and tried to draw her arm into his. A loud shout from the multitude of boys echoed through the darkened air. Hardly knowing what she did, she pressed through the crowd, and, breathless with fright, arrived at her home. And I will assure you she did not wish to take any more evening walks without a protector. From that time afterwards she was careful to be under her father's roof before it was dark.

Now can you think that your father or mother is unkind, because they are unwilling to have you placed in such a situation? And when they are doing all that they can to make you happy, ought you not to be grateful, and by a cheerful countenance, and ready obedience, to try to reward them for their love?

It is the duty of all children to keep in mind that their parents know what is best. And when they refuse to gratify your wishes, you should remember that their object is to do you good. That obedience, which is prompt and cheerful, is the only obedience which is acceptable to them, or well-pleasing to God. A great many cases will occur in which you will wish to do that which your parents will not approve. If you do not, in such cases, pleasantly and readily yield to their wishes, you are ungrateful and disobedient.

Neither is it enough that you should obey their expressed commands. You ought to try to do every thing which you think will give them pleasure, whether they tell you to do it or not. A good child will seek for opportunities to make his parents happy. A little girl, for instance, has some work to do. She knows that if she does it well and quick, it will gratify her mother. Now, if she be a good girl, she will not wait for her mother's orders, but will, of her own accord, improve her time, that she may exhibit the work to her mother sooner and more nicely done than she expected. Perhaps her mother is sick. Her affectionate daughter will not wait for her mother to express her wishes. She will try to anticipate them. She will walk softly around the chamber, arranging every thing in cheerful order. She will adjust the clothes of the bed that her mother may lay as comfortably as possible. And she will watch all her mother's movements that she may learn what things she needs before she asks for them. Such will be the conduct of an affectionate and obedient child.

I was once called to see a poor woman who was very sick. She was a widow, and in poverty. Her only companion and only earthly reliance was her daughter. As I entered the humble dwelling of this poor woman, I saw her bolstered up in the bed, with her pale countenance emaciated with pain, and every thing about the room proclaiming the most abject poverty. Her daughter sat sewing at the head of the bed, watching every want of her mother, and active with her needle. The perfect neatness of the room told how faithful the daughter in the discharge of her painful and arduous duties was. But her own slender form and consumptive countenance showed that by toil and watching she was almost worn out herself. This noble girl, by night and by day, with unwearied attention, endeavored to alleviate the excruciating pains of her afflicted parent. I could not look upon her but with admiration, in seeing the devotedness with which she watched every movement of her mother. How many wealthy parents would give all they possess, to be blessed with such a child! For months this devoted girl had watched around her mother by night and by day, with a care which seemed never to be weary. You could see by the movement of her eye, and by the expression of her countenance, how full her heart was of sympathy. She did not wait for her mother to tell her what to do, but was upon the watch all the time to find out what would be a comfort to her. This is what I call obedience. It is that obedience which God in heaven approves and loves.

I called often upon this poor widow, and always with increasing admiration of this devoted child. One morning, as I entered the room, I saw the mother lying upon the bed on the floor, with her head in the lap of her daughter. She was breathing short and heavy in the struggles of death. The tears were rolling down the pale cheeks of her daughter, as she pressed her hand upon the brow of her dying mother. The hour of death had just arrived, and the poor mother, in the triumphs of Christian faith, with faint and faltering accents, was imploring God's blessing upon her dear daughter. It was a most affecting farewell. The mother, while thus expressing her gratitude to God for the kindness of her beloved child, breathed her last. And angels must have looked upon that humble abode, and upon that affecting scene, with emotions of pleasure, which could hardly be exceeded by any thing else which the world could present. O that all children would feel the gratitude which this girl felt for a mother's early love! Then would the world be divested of half its sorrows, and of half its sins. This is the kind of obedience which every child should cultivate. You should

59

not only do whatever your parents tell you to do, with cheerfulness and alacrity, but you should be obedient to their wishes. You should be watching for opportunities to give them pleasure. You should, at all times, and under all circumstances, do every thing in your power to relieve them from anxiety and to make them happy. Then can you hope for the approbation of your God, and your heart will be filled with a joy which the ungrateful child can never feel. You can reflect with pleasure upon your conduct. When your parents are in the grave, you will feel no remorse of conscience harrowing your soul for your past unkindness. And when you die yourselves, you can anticipate a happy meeting with your parents, in that heavenly home, where sin and sorrow, and sickness and death, can never come.

God has, in almost every case, connected suffering with sin. And there are related many cases in which he has, in this world, most signally punished ungrateful children. I read a short time ago, an account of an old man, who had a drunken and brutal son. He would abuse his aged father without mercy. One day, he, in a passion, knocked him flat upon the floor, and, seizing him by his gray hairs, dragged him across the room to the threshold of the door, to cast him out. The old man, with his tremulous voice, cried out to his unnatural son, "It is enough—it is enough. God is just. When I was young, I dragged my own father in the same way; and now God is giving me the punishment I deserve."

Sometimes you will see a son who will not be obedient to his mother. He will have his own way, regardless of his mother's feelings. He has grown up to be a stout and stubborn boy, and now the ungrateful wretch will, by his misconduct, break the heart of that very mother, who, for months and years, watched over him with a care which knew no weariness. I call him a *wretch*, for I can hardly conceive of more enormous iniquity. That boy, or that young man, who does not treat his affectionate mother with kindness and respect, is worse than I can find language to describe. Perhaps you say, your mother is at times unreasonable. Perhaps she is, but what of that? You have been unreasonable ten thousand times, and she has borne with you and loved you. And even if your mother be at times unreasonable in her requirements, I want to know with what propriety you find fault with it. Is she to bear with all your cries in infancy, and all your fretfulness in childhood, and all your ingratitude and wants till you arrive at years of discretion, and then, because she wishes you to do some little thing which does not exactly meet your views, are you to turn upon her like a viper and sting her to the heart? The time was, when you were a little infant, your mother brought paleness to her own cheek, and weakness to her own frame, that she might give you support. You were sick, and in the cold winter night she would sit lonely by the fire, denying herself rest that she might lull her babe to sleep. You would cry with pain, and hour after hour she would walk the floor, carrying you in her arms, till her arms seemed ready to drop, and her limbs would hardly support her, through excess of weariness. The bright sun and the cloudless sky would invite her to go out for health and enjoyment, but she would deny herself the pleasure, and stay at home to take care of you, her helpless babe. Her friends would solicit her to indulge in the pleasures of the social evening party, but she would refuse for your sake and, in the solitude of her chamber, she would pass weeks and months watching all your wants. Thus have years passed away in which you have received nothing but kindness from her hands; and can you be so hard-hearted, so ungrateful, as now to give her one moment of unnecessary pain? If she has faults, can you not bear with them, when she has so long borne with you? Oh, if you knew but the hundredth part of what she has suffered and endured for your sake, you could not, *could not* be such a wretch as to requite her with ingratitude. A boy, who has one particle of generosity glowing in his bosom, will cling to his mother with an affection which life alone can extinguish. He will never let her have a single want which he can prevent. And when he grows to be a man, he will give her the warmest seat by his fireside and the choicest food upon his table. If necessary, he will deprive himself of comforts, that he may cheer her declining years. He will prove, by actions which cannot be misunderstood, that he feels a gratitude for a mother's love, which shall never, never leave him. And when she goes down to the grave in death, he will bedew her grave with the honorable tears of manly feeling. The son who does not feel thus, is unworthy of a mother's love; the frown of his offended Maker must be upon him, and he must render to Him an awful account for his ungrateful conduct.

It is, if possible, stranger still, that any *daughter* can forget a mother's care. You are always at home. You see your mother's solicitude. You are familiar with her heart. If you ever treat your mother with unkindness, remember that the time may come when your own heart will be broken by the misconduct of those who will be as dear to you as your mother's children are to her. And you may ask yourself whether you would be pleased with an exhibition of ungrateful feeling from a child whom you had loved and cherished with the tenderest care. God may reward you, even in this world, according to your deeds. And if he does not, he certainly will in the world to come. A day of judgment is at hand, and the ungrateful child has as fearful an account to render as any one who will stand at that bar.

I have just spoken to you of the grateful girl who took such good care of her poor sick mother. When that good girl dies, and meets her mother in heaven, what a happy meeting it will be! With how much joy will she reflect upon her dutifulness as a child! And as they dwell together again in the celestial mansions, sorrow and sighing will for ever flee away. If you wish to be happy here or hereafter, honor your father and your mother. Let love's pure flame burn in your heart and animate your life. Be brave, and fear not to do your duty. Be magnanimous, and do more for your parents than they require or expect. Resolve that you will do every thing in your power to make them happy, and you will be blessed as a child and useful and respected in your more mature years. Oh, how lovely is that son or daughter who has a grateful heart, and who will rather die than give a mother sorrow! Such a one is not only loved by all upon earth, but by the angels above, and by our Father in heaven.

It may assist you a little to estimate your obligations to your parents, to inquire what would become of you if your parents should refuse to take care of you any longer. You, at times, perhaps, feel unwilling to obey them: suppose they should say,

"Very well, my child, if you are unwilling to obey us, you may go away from home, and take care of yourself. We cannot be at the trouble and expense of taking care of you unless you feel some gratitude."

"Well," perhaps you would say, "let me have my cloak and bonnet, and I will go immediately."

"*Your cloak and bonnet!*" your mother would reply. "The cloak and bonnet are not yours, but your father's. He bought them and paid for them. Why do you call them yours?"

You might possibly reply, after thinking a moment, "They are mine because you gave them to me."

"No, my child," your mother would say, "we have only let you have them to wear. You never have paid a cent for them. You have not even paid us for the use of them. We wish to keep them for those of our children who are grateful for our kindness. Even the clothes you now have on are not yours. We will, however, give them to you; and now suppose you should go, and see how you can get along in taking care of yourself."

You rise to leave the house without any bonnet or cloak. But your mother says, "Stop one moment. Is there not an account to be settled before you leave? We have now clothed and boarded you for ten years. The trouble and expense, at the least calculation, amount to two dollars a week. Indeed, I do not suppose that you could have got any one else to have taken you so cheap. Your board, for ten years, at two dollars a week, amounts to one thousand and forty dollars. Are you under no obligation to us for all this trouble and expense?"

You hang down your head and do not know what to say. What can you say? You have no money. You cannot pay them.

Your mother, after waiting a moment for an answer, continues, "In many cases, when a person does not pay what is justly due, he is sent to jail. We, however, will be particularly kind to you, and wait awhile. Perhaps you can, by working for fifteen or twenty years, and by being very economical, earn enough to pay us. But let me see; the interest of the money will be over sixty dollars a year. Oh, no! It is out of the question. You probably could not earn enough to pay us in your whole life. We never shall be paid for the time, expense, and care, we have devoted to our ungrateful daughter. We hoped she would love us, and obey us, and thus repay. But it seems she prefers to be ungrateful and disobedient. Good bye."

You open the door and go out. It is cold and windy. Shivering with the cold, and without money, you are at once a beggar, and must perish in the streets, unless some one takes pity on you.

You go, perhaps, to the house of a friend, and ask if they will allow you to live with them.

They at once reply, "We have so many children of our own, that we cannot afford to take you, unless you will pay for your board and clothing."

You go again out into the street, cold, hungry, and friendless. The darkness of the night is coming on; you have no money to purchase a supper, or night's lodging. Unless you can get some employment, or find some one who will pity you, you must lie down upon the hard ground, and perish with hunger and with cold.

Perhaps some benevolent man sees you as he is going home in the evening, and takes you to the overseers of the poor, and says, "Here is a little vagrant girl I found in the streets. We must send the poor little thing to the poor house, or she will starve to death."

You are carried to the poor house. There you find a very different home from your father's. You are dressed in the coarsest garments. You have the vilest food, and are compelled to be obedient, and to do the most servile work.

Now, suppose, while you are in the poor house, some kind gentleman and lady should come and say, "We will take this little girl, and give her food and clothes for nothing. We will take her into our own parlor, and give her a chair by our own pleasant fireside. We will buy every thing for her that she needs. We will hire persons to teach her. We will do every thing in our power to make her happy, and will not ask for one cent of pay in return."

What should you think of such kindness? And what should you think of yourself, if you could go to their parlor, and receive their bounty, and yet be ungrateful and disobedient? Would not a child who could thus requite such love, be deserving of universal detestation? But all this your parents are doing, and for years have been doing for you. They pay for the fire that warms you; for the house that shelters you; for the clothes that cover you; for the food that supports you! They watch over your bed in sickness, and provide for your instruction and enjoyment when in health! Your parents do all this without money and without price. Now, whenever you feel ill humored, or disposed to murmur at any of their requirements, just look a moment and see how the account stands. Inquire what would be the consequence, if they should refuse to take care of you.

The child, who does not feel grateful for all this kindness, must be more unfeeling than the brutes. How can you refrain from doing every thing in your power to make those happy who have loved you so long, and have conferred upon you so many favors! If you have any thing noble or generous in your nature, it must be excited by a parent's love. You sometimes see a child who receives all these favors as though they were her due. She appears to have no consciousness of obligation; no heart of gratitude. Such a child is a disgrace to human nature. Even the very fowls of the air, and cattle of the fields, love their parents. They put to shame the ungrateful child.

You can form no conception of that devotedness of love which your mother cherishes for you. She is willing to suffer almost every thing to save you from pain. She will, to protect you, face death in its most terrific form. An

English gentleman tells the following affecting story, to show how ardently a mother loves her child.

"I was once going, in my gig, up the hill in the village of Frankford, near Philadelphia when a little girl about two years old, who had toddled away from a small house, was lying basking in the sun, in the middle of the road. About two hundred yards before I got to the child, the teams of three wagons, five big horses in each, the drivers of which had stopped to drink at a tavern at the brow of the hill, started off, and came nearly abreast, galloping down the road. I got my gig off the road as speedily as I could, but expected to see the poor child crushed to pieces. A young man, a journeyman carpenter, who was shingling a shed by the road side, seeing the child, and seeing the danger, though a stranger to the parents, jumped from the top of the shed, ran into the road, and snatched up the child from scarcely an inch before the hoof of the leading horse. The horse's leg knocked him down; but he, catching the child by its clothes, flung it back out of the way of the other horses, and saved himself by rolling back with surprising agility. The mother of the child, who had apparently been washing, seeing the teams coming, and seeing the situation of the child, rushed out, and, catching up the child, just as the carpenter had flung it back, and hugging it in her arms, uttered a shriek, such as I never heard before, never heard since, and, I hope, shall never hear again; and then she dropped down as if perfectly dead. By the application of the usual means, she was restored, however, in a little while, and I, being about to depart, asked the carpenter if he were a married man, and whether he were a relation of the parents of the child. He said he was neither. 'Well, then,' said I, 'you merit the gratitude of every father and mother in the world, and I will show you mine by giving you what I have,—pulling out the nine or ten dollars which I had in my pocket. 'No, I thank you, sir,' said he, 'I have only done what it was my duty to do.'

"Bravery, disinterestedness, and maternal affection surpassing these it is impossible to imagine. The mother was going right in amongst the feet of these powerful and wild horses, and amongst the wheels of the wagons. She had no thought for herself; no feeling of fear for her own life; her *shriek* was the sound of inexpressible joy, joy too great for her to support herself under."

Now, can you conceive a more ungrateful wretch, than that boy would be, if he should grow up, not to love or obey his mother? She was willing to die for him. She was willing to run directly under the feet of those ferocious horses, that she might save his life. And if he has one particle of generosity in his bosom, he will do every thing in his power to make her happy.

But your mother loves you as well as did that mother love her child. She is as willing to expose herself to danger and to death. And can you ever bear the thought of causing grief to her whose love is so strong; whose kindness is so great? It does appear to me that the generous-hearted boy, who thinks of these things, will resolve to be his mother's joy and blessing.

A few years ago a child was lost in one of those vast plains in the west, called prairies. A gentleman, who was engaged in the search for the child, thus describes the scene. It forcibly shows the strength of a mother's love.

"In the year 1821 I was stationed on the Mad River circuit. You know there are extensive prairies in that part of the state. In places, there are no dwellings within miles of each other; and animals of prey are often seen there. One evening, late in autumn, a few of the neighbors were assembled around me, in one of those solitary dwellings, and we had got well engaged in the worship of God, when it was announced that the child of a widow was lost in the prairie. It was cold; the wind blew; and some rain was falling. The poor woman was in agony, and our meeting was broken up. All prepared to go in search of the lost child. The company understood the business better than I did, for they had been bred in those extensive barrens; and occurrences like the present are, probably, not infrequent among them. They equipped themselves with lanterns and torches, for it was quite dark; and tin horns, to give signals to different parts of the company, when they should become widely separated. For my part, I thought duty required that I should take charge of the unhappy mother. She was nearly frantic; and as time permitted her to view her widowed and childless condition, and the circumstances of the probable death of her child, her misery seemed to double upon her. She took my arm; the company divided into parties; and, taking different directions, we commenced the search. The understanding was, that, when the child should be found, a certain wind of the horn should be made, and that all who should hear it should repeat the signal. In this way all the company would receive the information.

"The prospect of finding a lost child in those extensive prairies, would, at any time, be sufficiently discouraging. The difficulty must be greatly increased by a dark, rainy night. We traveled many miles, and to a late hour. At length we became satisfied that further search would be unavailing; and all but the mother determined to return home. It was an idea she could not, for a moment, endure. She would hear of nothing but further search. Her strength, at last, began to fail her, and I prevailed on her to return to her abode. As she turned her face from further search, and gave up her child as lost, her misery was almost too great for endurance. 'My child,' said she, 'has been devoured by a wild beast; his little limbs have been torn asunder; and his blood been drunk by the hideous monster,'—and the idea was agony. As she clung to my arm, it seemed as if her heart-strings would break. At times I had almost to support her in my arms, to prevent her falling to the earth.

"As we proceeded on our way back, I thought I heard, at a great distance, the sound of a horn. We stopped, and listened; it was repeated. It was the concerted signal. The child was found. And what were the feelings of the mother!" Language cannot describe them. Such is the strength of maternal affection. And can a child be so hard-hearted as not to love a mother? Is there any thing which can be more ungrateful than to grieve one who loves you so ardently, and who has done so much for you?

If there be any crime which in the sight of God is greater than all others, it appears to me it must be the abuse of parents. If the spirit of a demon dwells in any human breast, it must be in that breast which is thankless for parental favors, and which can requite that love, which watched over our infancy and protected our helpless years, with ingratitude and disrespect.

Chapter Five

Religious Truth

In this chapter I shall take up the subject of religion. That you may understand your duties, it is important that you should first understand your own character in the sight of God. I can, perhaps, make this plain to you by the following illustration:

A few years ago a ship sailed from England to explore the Northern Ocean. As it was a voyage of no common danger to face the storms and the tempests of those icy seas, a crew of experienced seamen was obtained, and placed under the guidance of a commander of long-tried skill. As the ship sailed from an English port, in pleasant weather and with favorable breezes, all was harmony on board, and every man was obedient to the lawful commander. As weeks passed away, and they pressed forward on the wide waste of waters, there were occasional acts of neglect of duty. Still the commander retained his authority. No one ventured to refuse to be in subjection to him. But as the ship advanced farther and farther into those unexplored regions, new toils and dangers stared them in the face. The cold blasts of those wintry regions chilled their limbs. Mountains of ice, dashed about by the tempests, threatened destruction to the ship and to the crew. As far as the eye could reach, a dreary view of chilling waves and of floating ice warned them of dangers, from which no earthly power could extricate them. The ship was far away from home, and in regions which had been seldom, if ever, seen by mortal eyes. The boldest were at times horrified by the dangers, both seen and unseen, which were clustering around them. Under these circumstances the spirit of revolt broke out among that ship's crew. They resolved that they would no longer be in subjection to their commander. They rose together in rebellion; deprived him of his authority, and took the control of the ship into their own hands. They then placed their captain in an open boat and throwing in to him a few articles of provision, they turned him adrift upon that wide and cheerless ocean, and he never was heard of again. Appointing one of their number as commander, they turned the ship in a different direction, and regulated all their movements by their own pleasure. After this revolt, things went on pretty much as before. They had deprived their *lawful* commander of his authority and elevated another to occupy his place. A stranger would, perhaps, have perceived no material difference, after this change, in the conduct of the crew. The preservation of their own lives rendered it necessary that the established rules of naval discipline should be observed. By night the watches were regularly set and relieved as before. The helmsman performed his accustomed duty, and the sails were spread to the winds, or furled in the tempest, as occasion required. But still they were all guilty of mutiny. They had refused to submit to their lawful commander. Consequently, by the laws of their country, they were all condemned to be hung. The faithful discharge of the necessary duties of each day after their revolt, did not in the least free them from blame. The crime of which they were guilty, and for which they deserved the severest punishment, was the refusal to submit to authority.

Now, our situation is very similar to that of this rebellious crew. The Bible tells us that we have said in our hearts that "we will not have God to reign over us."[14] Instead of living in entire obedience to him, we have chosen to serve ourselves. The accusation which God has against us is not that we occasionally transgress his laws, but that we refuse to regard him, at all times and under all circumstances, as our ruler. Sometimes children think that if they do not tell lies, and if they obey their parents, it is all that God requires of them. This, however, is by no means the case. God requires of us not only to do our duty to our parents, and to those around us, but also to love him with our most ardent affection, and to endeavor at all times to do that which will be pleasing to him. While the mutinous seamen had command of the ship, they might have been kind to one another; they might, with unwearied care and attention, have watched over the sick. They might, with the utmost fidelity, have conformed to the rules of naval discipline, seeing that every rope was properly adjusted, and that cleanliness and order should pervade every department. But notwithstanding all this, their guilt was undiminished. They had refused obedience to their commander, and for this they were exposed to the penalty of that law which doomed them to death.

It is the same with us. We may be kind to one another; we may be free from guile; we may be faithful in the discharge of the ordinary duties of life; yet, if we are not in subjection to God, we are justly exposed to the penalty of his law. What would have been thought of one of those mutinous seamen, if, when brought before the bar

---

[14] Compare Psalm 2 with Luke 19:14.

of his country, he had pleaded in his defense, that, after the revolt, he had been faithful to his new commander? Would any person have regarded that as an extenuation[15] of his sin? No! He would at once have been led to the scaffold. And the voice of an indignant public would have said that he suffered justly for his crime.

Let us imagine one of the mutineers in a court of justice, and urging the following excuses to the judge.

Judge—You have been accused of mutiny, and are found guilty; and now what have you to say why sentence of death should not be pronounced against you?

Criminal—To be sure I did help place the captain in the boat and turn him adrift; but then I was no worse than the others. I did only as the rest did.

Judge—The fact that others were equally guilty, is no excuse for you. You are to be judged by your own conduct.

Criminal—Well, it is very unjust that I should be punished, for I was one of the hardest-working men on board the ship. No one can say that they ever saw me idle, or that I ever refused to perform any duty, however dangerous.

Judge—You are not on trial for idleness, but for *refusing obedience to your commander.*

Criminal—I was a very moral man. No one ever heard me use a profane word; and in my conduct and actions, I was civil to all my shipmates.

Judge—You are not accused of profanity, or of impoliteness. The charge, for which you are arraigned, is that you have rebelled against lawful authority. Of this you

---

[15] The act of extenuating or the state of being extenuated; the act of making thin, slender, or lean, or of palliating; diminishing, or lessening; palliation, as of a crime; mitigation, as of punishment.

have been proved to be guilty; and for this I must now proceed to pass the penalty of the law.

Criminal—But, may it please your honor, I was a very benevolent man. One night one of my shipmates was sick, and I watched all the night long at his hammock. And after we placed the captain in the boat, and cut him adrift, I threw in a bag of biscuit, that he might have some food.

Judge—If your benevolence had shown itself in defending your commander, and in obedience to his authority, you might now be rewarded; but you are guilty of mutiny, and must be hung.

Criminal—There was no man on board the ship more useful than I was. And after we had turned the captain adrift, we must all have perished if it had not been for me, for no one else understood navigation. I have a good education, and did every thing I could to instruct my shipmates, and to make them skilful seamen.

Judge—You are then the most guilty of the whole rebellious crew. You knew your duty better than the rest, and are more inexcusable in not being faithful. It appears by your own confession, that your education was good; that your influence was extensive; and that you had been taught those duties which man owes his fellow man. This does not extenuate, but increases your guilt. Many of your shipmates were ignorant, and were confirmed in their rebellion by your example. They had never been taught those moral and social duties which had been impressed upon your mind. That you could have been so ungrateful, so treacherous, so cruel as to engage in this revolt, justly exposes you to the severest penalty of the law. I therefore proceed to pronounce upon you the sentence which your crimes deserve. You will be led from this place to the deepest and strongest dungeon of the prison; there to be confined till you are led to the gallows, and there to be hung by the neck till you are dead; and may God have mercy upon your soul.

Now, who would not declare that this sentence is just? And who does not see the absurdity of the excuses which the guilty man offered?

So it is with you, my young reader. It is your duty, at all times, to be obedient to God. The charge which God brings against us, is, that we have refused to obey him. For this we deserve that penalty which God has threatened against rebellion. If we love our parents ever so ardently, it will not save us, unless we also love God. If we are ever so kind to those around us, it will not secure God's approbation, unless we are also obedient to him. If our conduct is so correct that no one can accuse us of what is called an immoral act, it will be of no avail, unless we are also living with faith in the promises of God, and with persevering efforts to do his will. And we shall be as foolish as was the guilty mutineer, if we expect that any such excuses will save us from the penalty of his law.

We cannot, by any fidelity in the discharge of the common duties of life, atone for the neglect to love and serve our Maker. We have broken away from his authority. We follow our own inclinations, and are obedient to the directions of others, rather than to those of our Maker. The fact is, that the duties we owe God and our fellow men are not to be separated. God expects the child in the morning to acknowledge his dependence upon his Maker, and to pray for assistance to do that which is right, during all the hours of the day. And he expects you, when the evening comes, to thank him for all his goodness, and solemnly to promise, all your days, to be obedient to his authority. You must not only love your parents, but you must also love your God. You must try to have your words and your thoughts pure, and all your conduct holy. Now, when you look back upon your past lives, and when you examine your present feelings, do you not see that you have not obeyed God in all your ways? Not only have you had wicked thoughts, and at times been disobedient to your parents, but you have not made it the great object of your life to serve your Maker.

God now desires to have you obedient to him. He loves you, and wishes to see you happy. He has for this purpose sent his Son into the world to die for your sins, and to lead you to piety and peace. The Savior now asks you to repent of sin and love him, that, when you die, you may be received to heaven, and be happy for ever. You perhaps remember the passage of Scripture, "Behold, I stand at the door, and knock; if any man hear my voice, and open the door, I will come in to him, and sup with him, and he with me."[16] By this our Lord expresses his desire that we should receive him to our hearts.

One of the most affecting scenes described by the pen of the most eloquent of writers, is, that of an aged father driven from his home by ungrateful and hard-hearted children. The broken-hearted man is represented as standing by the door of his own house, in a dark and tempestuous night, with his gray locks streaming in the wind, and his head unprotected to the fury of the storm. There he stands, drenched with the rain, and shivering with the cold. But the door is barred, and the shutters are closed. His daughters hear the trembling voice of their aged parent, but refuse him admission. Their flinty hearts remain unmoved. The darkness increases; the tempest rages; the rain falls in torrents, and the wind howls most fearfully. The voice of their father grows feebler and feebler, as the storm spends its fury upon him. But nothing

---

[16] Revelation 3:20.

can touch the sympathies of his unnatural children. They will not open the door to him. At last, grief, and the pangs of disappointed hope, breaks the father's heart. He looks at the black and lowering clouds above him, and, in the frenzy of his distracted mind, invites the increasing fury of the storm. And still those wretched children refuse to receive him to their fireside, but leave him to wander in the darkness and the cold.

The representation of this scene, as described by the pen of Shakespeare, has brought tears into millions of eyes. The tragedy of King Lear and his wretched daughters is known throughout the civilized world. What heart is not indignant at such treatment? Who does not abhor the conduct of these unnatural children?

Our blessed Savior represents himself as taking a similar attitude before the hearts of his children. He has presented himself at the door of your heart, and can you refuse him admission? "Behold," says he, "I stand at the door and knock." But we, with a hardness of heart which has triumphed over greater blessings, and is consequently more inexcusable than that of the daughters of King Lear, refuse to love him, and to receive him as our friend. He entreats admission. He asks to enter and be with you and you with him, that you may be happy. And there he has stood for days, and months, and years, and you receive him not. Could we see our own conduct in the light in which we behold the conduct of others, we should be confounded with the sense of our guilt.

Is there a child who reads this book, who has not at times felt the importance of loving the Savior? When you felt these serious impressions, Christ was pleading for admission to your heart. You have, perhaps, been sick, and feared that you were about to die. And, oh, how ardently did you then wish that the Savior were your friend!

Perhaps you have seen a brother or a sister die: you wept over your companion, as her cheek daily grew paler, and she drew nearer and nearer to death. And when she ceased to breathe, and her limbs were cold and lifeless, you wept as though your heart would break. And when you saw her placed in the coffin and carried to the grave, how earnestly did you desire to be prepared to die yourself! Oh, how did the world seem then to you! This was the way the Savior took to reach your heart. When on earth, he said, "Suffer little children to come unto me, and forbid them not."[17] And now he endeavors, in many ways, to induce you to turn to him. Sometimes he makes you happy, that his goodness may excite your love. When he sees that in happiness you are most prone to forget him, he sends sorrow and trouble, under which your spirits sink, and this world appears gloomy, and you are led to look forward to a happier one to come. And does it not seem very ungrateful that you should resist all this kindness and care, and continue to refuse to submit yourself to him? You think the daughters of King Lear were very cruel. Indeed they were; but not as cruel as you. Their father had been kind to them, but not as kind as your Savior has been to you. He stood long at the door and knocked, but not so long as the Savior has stood at the door of your heart. It is in vain that we look to find an instance of ingratitude equal to that manifested by the sinner who rejects the Savior. And it is, indeed, melancholy to think, that any child could be so hard-hearted.

It is strange that any person can resist the love which God has manifested for us. He has sent angels with messages of mercy, and invitations to his home in heaven. He sent his Son to die that we might be saved from

---

[17] Matthew 19:14; Mark 10:14; Luke 18:16.

everlasting sorrow. He has provided a world of beauty and of glory, far surpassing any thing we can conceive, to which he invites us, and where he will make us happy for ever. And we are informed that all the angels in heaven are so much interested in our welfare, that "there is joy in the presence of the angels of God over one sinner that repenteth."[18] It is indeed wonderful that the holy and happy angels above should feel so deep an interest in our concerns. But, oh, how surpassingly strange it is, that we feel so little for ourselves!

It is kind in God that he will not let the wicked enter heaven. He loves his holy children there too well, to allow the wicked to enter and trouble them, and destroy their peace. There was a little girl once, who had a party of her companions to spend the evening with her. They were all playing very happily in the parlor, when a drunken man happened to go by. As he heard their voices, he came staggering up to the door, and tried to get in. All the girls were very much frightened, for fear the degraded wretch would get into the parlor. But the gentleman of the house told them not to be frightened. He assured them that the man should not come in, and though it was a cold winter's night, he went out and drove him away. Now, was not this gentleman kind thus to protect these children?

Suppose a wicked man or a lost spirit should go to the gates of heaven and try to enter there. Do you suppose that God would let him in? Would not God be as kind to the angels as an earthly father to his earthly children? Every angel in heaven would cry to God for protection, if they should see the wicked approaching that happy world. And God shows his love, by declaring that the wicked shall never enter there.

---

[18] Luke 15:10.

"These holy gates for ever bar
Pollution, sin and shame;
None shall obtain admittance there,
But followers of the Lamb."

It is not because God is unkind and cruel that he shuts up the wicked in the world of woe. He does this because he loves his children, and, like a kind father, determines to protect them from oppression and sorrow. The bright wings of the angel glitter in the heavenly world. Pure joy glows in the bosoms of the blest. Love unites them all, as they swell their songs, and take their flight. In their home, the wicked cease from troubling, and the weary are for ever at rest.

A few years ago, there was a certain family which was united and happy. The father and mother looked upon the children who surrounded their fireside, and beheld them all virtuous in their conduct, and affectionate towards one another. Their evening sports went on harmoniously, and those children were preparing, in their beloved home, for future virtues and usefulness. But, at last, one of the sons became dissipated. He went on from step to step in vice, till he became a degraded wretch. His father and mother wept over his sins, and did every thing in their power to reclaim him. All was in vain. Every day he grew worse. His brothers and sisters found all the happiness of their home destroyed by his wickedness. The family was disgraced by him, and they were all in sorrow and tears. One evening he was brought home so intoxicated that he was apparently lifeless. His poor broken-hearted mother saw him carried in this disgraceful condition to his bed. At another time, when his parents were absent, he came home, in the evening, in a state of intoxication bordering on delirium. He raved about the house like a madman. He swore the most shocking oaths. Enraged with one of his sisters, he seized a chair, and would have struck her, perhaps, a fatal blow, if she had not escaped by flight. The parents of this child felt that such things could no longer be permitted, and told him that, if there was not an immediate reformation in his conduct, they would forbid him to enter their house. But entreaties and warnings were alike in vain. He continued his disgraceful career. His father, perceiving that amendment was hopeless, and that he was, by remaining at home, embittering every moment of the family, and loading them with disgrace, sent his son to sea, and told him never to return till he could come back improved in character. To protect his remaining children, it was necessary for him to send the dissolute one away.

Now, was this father cruel, in thus endeavoring to promote the peace and the happiness of his family? Was it unkind in him to resolve to make his virtuous children happy, by excluding the vicious and the degraded? No! Everyone sees that this is the principal of paternal love. If he had been a cruel father—if he had had no regard for his children, he would have allowed this abandoned son to have remained, and behaved as he pleased. He would have made no effort to protect his children, and to promote their joy and blessedness.

And is it not kind in our heavenly Father to resolve that those who will not obey his laws shall be for ever excluded from heaven? He loves his virtuous and obedient children, and will make them perfectly happy. He never will permit the wicked to mar their joys and degrade their home. If God were an unkind being, he would let the wicked go to heaven. He would have no prison to detain them. He would leave the good unprotected and exposed to abuse from the bad. But God is love. He never thus will abandon his children. He has provided a strong prison, with dungeons deep and dark, where he will hold the wicked, so that they cannot escape. The angels in heaven have nothing to fear from wicked men, or wicked angels. God will protect his children from all harm.

Our Father in heaven is now inviting all of us to repent of our sins, and to cultivate a taste for the joys of heaven. He wishes to take us to his own happy home, and make us loved members of his own affectionate family. And every angel in heaven rejoices, when he sees the humblest child repent of sin and turn to God. But if we will not be obedient to his laws; if we will not cultivate in our hearts those feelings of fervent love which glow and burn in the angel's bosom; if we will not here on earth learn the language of prayer and praise, God assures us that we never can be admitted to mingle with his happy family above. Would not God be very unkind to allow the wicked and impenitent to enter in and mar their joys? The angels are happy to welcome a returning wanderer. But if they should see an unsubdued spirit directing his flight towards heaven, they all would pray to God that he might not be permitted to enter, to throw discord into their songs, and sorrow into their hearts. God is love. He will keep heaven pure and happy. All who will be obedient to him, he will gladly elevate to walk the streets of the New Jerusalem, and to inhabit the mansions which he has built.

But those who will not submit to his authority must be shut out for ever. If we do not yield to the warnings and entreaties which now come to us from God, we must hear the sentence, "Depart from me,"—"I know you not."[19] God uses all the means which he deems proper to reclaim

---

[19] Matthew 7:23.

us; and when he finds that we are incorrigible, then does he close upon us the doors of our prison, that we never may escape.

If God cared not for the happiness of his children, he would break these laws; he would tear down this prison; he would turn all its guilty inmates loose upon the universe, to rove and to desolate at their pleasure. But, blessed be God, he is love; and the brightness and glory of heaven never can be marred by the entrance of sin. In hell's dreary abyss, the wretched outcasts from heaven will find their secure and eternal abiding place. Where do you wish to have your home? with the virtuous and happy in heaven, or with the vicious and miserable in the world of woe? Now is the time to decide. But life will soon be gone. As we die, we shall continue for ever.

> "There are no acts of pardon passed
> In the cold grave to which we haste."

God, in this world, makes use of all those means which he thinks calculated to affect your feelings and to incline you to his service. You now hear of the love of Jesus, and feel the strivings of the Holy Spirit. You are surrounded by many who love the Savior, and enjoy all the precious privileges of the Bible and the Sabbath. God speaks to you in afflictions and enjoyments, and tries ways without number to reclaim you to himself. If you can resist all this, your case is hopeless. In the world of woe there will be no one to plead with you the wonders of a Savior's love. You will feel no strivings of the Spirit. No Christian friends will surround you with their sympathies and their prayers. The Sabbath will no longer dawn upon you, and the Bible will no longer entreat you to turn to the Lord. If you can resist all the motives to repentance which this life affords, you are proof against all the means which God sees fit to adopt. If you die impenitent, you will for ever remain impenitent, and go on unrestrained in passion and woe. The word of God has declared that, at the Day of Judgment our doom will be fixed for ever. The wicked shall then go into everlasting punishment and the righteous to life eternal. The bars of the sinner's prison will never be broken. The glories of the saint's abode will never be sullied.

A few years ago, a child was lost in the woods. He was out, with his brothers and sisters, gathering berries, and accidentally was separated from them and lost. The children, after looking in vain for some time in search of the little wanderer, returned just in the dusk of the evening, to inform their parents that their brother was lost, and could not be found. The woods at that time were infested with bears. The darkness of a cloudy night was rapidly coming on, and the alarmed father, gathering a few of his neighbors, hastened in search of the lost child. The mother remained at home, almost distracted with suspense. As the clouds gathered and the darkness increased, the father and the neighbors, with highly-excited fears, traversed the woods in all directions, and raised loud shouts to attract the attention of the child. But their search was in vain. They could find no traces of the wanderer; and as they stood under the boughs of the lofty trees, and listened, that if possible they might hear his feeble voice, no sound was borne to their ears but the melancholy moaning of the wind as it swept through the thick branches of the forest. The gathering clouds threatened an approaching storm, and the deep darkness of the night had already enveloped them. It is difficult to conceive what were the feelings of that father. And who could imagine how deep the agony which filled the bosom of that mother as she heard the wind, and beheld the darkness in which her child was wandering! The search continued in vain till nine o'clock in the evening. Then one of the party was sent back to the village to collect the inhabitants for a more extensive search. The bell rung the alarm, and the cry of fire resounded through the streets. It was, however, ascertained that it was not fire which caused the alarm, but that the bell tolled the more solemn tidings of a lost child. Every heart sympathized in the sorrows of the distracted parents. Soon the multitudes of the people were seen ascending the hill upon the declivity of which the village was situated, to aid in the search. Ere long the rain began to fall, but no tidings came back to the village of the lost child. Hardly an eye was that night closed in sleep, and there was not a mother who did not feel for the agonized parents. The night passed away, and the morning dawned, and yet no tidings came. At last those engaged in the search met together and held a consultation. They made arrangements for a more minute and extended search, and agreed that in case the child was found, a gun should be fired to give a signal to the rest of the party. As the sun arose, the clouds were dispelled, and the whole landscape glittered in the rays of the bright morning. But that village was deserted and still. The stores were closed, and business was hushed. Mothers were walking the streets with sympathizing countenances and anxious hearts. There was but one thought there—What has become of the lost child? All the affections and interest of the community were flowing in one deep and broad channel towards the little wanderer. About nine in the morning the signal gun was fired, which announced that the child was found; and for a moment how dreadful was the suspense! Was it found a mangled corpse, or was it alive and well? Soon a joyful shout proclaimed the safety of the child. The shout was borne from tongue to tongue, till the whole forest rung again with the joyful acclamations of the multitude. A commissioned messenger rapidly bore the tidings to the distracted mother. A procession was immediately formed by those engaged in the search. The child was placed upon a platform, hastily constructed from the boughs of trees, and borne in triumph at the head of the procession. When they arrived at the brow of the hill, they rested for a moment, and proclaimed their success with three loud and animated cheers. The procession then moved on, till they arrived in front of the dwelling where the parents of the child resided. The mother, who stood at the door, with streaming eyes and throbbing heart, could no longer restrain herself or her feelings. She rushed into the street, clasped her child to her bosom, and wept aloud. Every eye was suffused with tears, and for a moment all were silent. But suddenly some one gave a signal for a shout. One loud, and long, and happy note of joy rose from the assembled multitude, and they then dispersed to their business and their homes.

There was more joy over the one child that was found than over the ninety and nine that went not astray. Likewise there is joy in the presence of the angels of God over one sinner that repenteth. But still this is a feeble representation of the love of our Father in heaven for us, and of the joy with which the angels welcome the returning wanderer. The mother cannot feel for her child that is lost as God feels for the unhappy wanderers in the paths of sin. The child was exposed to a few hours of suffering; the sinner to eternal despair. The child was in danger of being torn by the claws and the teeth of the bear—a pang which would be but for a moment; but the sinner must feel the ravages of the never-dying worm, must be exposed to the fury of the inextinguishable flame.

Oh, if a mother can feel so much, what must be the feelings of our Father in heaven! If man can feel so deep a sympathy, what must be the emotions which glow in the bosoms of angels! Such is the nature of the feelings with which we are regarded by our heavenly Father and the holy angels.

Many parables are introduced in the Bible to illustrate this feeling on the part of God. He compares himself with the kind shepherd, who, finding that one little lamb had strayed from the flock, left the ninety and nine and went in search of the lost one. He illustrates this feeling by that of the woman who had lost a piece of silver, and immediately lit a candle and swept the house diligently, till she found it. In like manner, we are informed, that it is not the will of our Father who is in heaven, that one of his little ones should perish. He has manifested the most astonishing love and kindness that he might make us happy.

But what greater proof of love can we have than that which God has given in the gift of his Son! That you might be saved from sin and ceaseless woe, Jesus came and died. He came to the world, and placed himself in poverty, and was overwhelmed with sorrow, that he might induce you to accept salvation, and to be happy for ever in heaven. The Savior was born in a stable. When an infant, his life was sought. His parents were compelled to flee out of the country that they might save him from a violent death. As he grew up, he was friendless and forsaken. He went about from town to town, and from village to village, doing good to all. He visited the sick, and healed them. He went to the poor and the afflicted, and comforted them. He took little children in his arms, and blessed them. He injured no one, and endeavored to do good to all. And yet he was persecuted, and insulted, and abused. Again and again he was compelled to flee for his life. They took up stones to stone him. They hired false witnesses to accuse him. At last they took him by night, as he was in a garden praying. A cruel multitude came and took him by force, and carried him into a large hall. They then surrounded our blessed Savior, and heaped upon him all manner of insult and abuse. They mocked him. They collected some thorns, and made a crown, which they forced upon his head, pressing the sharp thorns into his flesh, till the blood flowed down upon his hair and his cheeks. And after thus passing the whole night, he was led out to the hill of Calvary, tottering beneath the heavy burden of the cross, which he was compelled to bear upon his own shoulders, and to which he was to be nailed. When they arrived at the place of crucifixion, they drove the nails through his hands and his feet. The cross was then fixed in the ground, and the Savior, thus cruelly suspended, was exposed to the loud and contemptuous shouts of an insulting mob. The morning air was filled with their loud execrations. A soldier came and thrust a spear deep into his side. To quench his burning thirst, they gave him vinegar, mixed with gall. Thus did our Savior die. He endured all this, from the cradle to the grave that he might save sinners. And when he, while enduring the agony of the cross, cried out, "My God, my God, why hast thou forsaken me?"[20] he was then suffering those sorrows which you must otherwise have suffered. If it had not been for our Savior's sorrows and death, there would have been no help for any sinner. You never could have entered heaven. You must for ever have endured the penalty of that law which saith, "The soul that sinneth, it shall die."[21] Was there ever such love as this? And, oh, must not that child's heart be hard,

---

[20] Matthew 27:46; Mark 15:34; cf. Psalm 22:1.
[21] Ezekiel 18:4,20.

who will not love such a Savior, and who will not do all in his power to prove his gratitude by a holy and an obedient life? Christ so loves you, that he was willing to die the most cruel of deaths, that he might make you happy. He is now in heaven, preparing mansions of glory for all those who will accept him as their Savior, and obey his law. And where is the child who does not wish to have this Savior for his friend, and to have a home in heaven?

The Holy Spirit is promised to aid you in all your efforts to resist sin. If, when the power of temptation is strong, you will look to him for aid, he will give you strength to resist. Thus is duty made easy. God loves you. Angels desire that you should come to heaven. Jesus has died to save sinners like you. The Holy Spirit is ready to aid you in every Christian effort, and to lead you on, victorious over sin. How unreasonable, then, and how ungrateful it is, for any child to refuse to love God, and to prepare to enter the angels' home! There you can be happy. No night is there. No sickness or sorrow can ever reach you there. Glory will fill your eye. Joy will fill your heart. You will be like an angel yourself,[22] and shine in all the purity and in all the bliss of the angels' happy home.

---

[22] Matthew 22:30; Mark 12:25; Luke 20:36.

Chapter Six

Piety

In the last chapter I have endeavored to show you in what your sin principally consists; and also the interest which God feels in your happiness, and the sacrifice he has made to lead you to penitence and to heaven. But you desire more particular information respecting the *duties* which God requires of you. I shall in this chapter explain the requirements of God; and show you why you should immediately commence a life of piety.

Probably no child reads this book that is not conscious of sin. You feel not only that you do not love God as you ought, but that sometimes you are ungrateful or disobedient to your parents; you are irritated with your brother or your sister, or you indulge in other feelings, which you know to be wrong. Now, the first thing which God requires of you is that you should be penitent for all your sins. At the close of the day, you go to your bed chamber for sleep. Perhaps your mother goes with you, and hears you repeat a prayer of gratitude to God for his kindness. But after she has left the chamber, and you are alone in the darkness, you recall to mind the events of the day, asking yourself what you have done that is wrong. Perhaps you were idle at school, or unkind to a playmate,

91

or disobedient to your parents. Now, if you go to sleep without sincere repentance, and a firm resolution to try for the future to avoid such sin, the frown of your Maker will be upon you during all the hours of the night. You ought, every evening, before you go to sleep, to think of your conduct during the day, and to express to God your sincere sorrow for every thing you have done which is displeasing to him, and humbly implore the pardon of your sins through Jesus Christ. Such a child God loves. Such a one he will readily forgive. And if it is his will that you should die before the morning, he will take you to heaven, to be happy there. But remember that it is not enough simply to *say* that you are penitent. You must really *feel* penitent. And you must resolve to be more watchful in the future, and to guard against the sin over which you mourn. You have, for instance, spoken unkindly, during the day, to your brother. At night, you feel that you have done wrong, and that God is displeased. Now, if you are sincerely penitent, and ask God's forgiveness, you will pray that you may not again be guilty of the same fault. And when you awake in the morning, you will be watchful over yourself, that you may be pleasant and obliging. You will perhaps go to your brother and say, "I did wrong in speaking unkindly to you yesterday, and I am sorry for it. I will endeavor never again to do so." At any rate, if you are really penitent, you will pray to God for forgiveness, and most sincerely resolve never willingly to be guilty of the same sin again.

But you must also remember that, by the law of God, sin can never pass unpunished. God has said, "The soul that sinneth, it shall die."[23] And when you do any thing that is wrong, and afterwards repent of it, God

---

[23] Ezekiel 18:4,20.

forgives you, because the Savior has borne the punishment which you deserve. This is what is meant by that passage of Scripture, "he was wounded for our transgressions, and bruised for our iniquities."[24] Our Father in heaven loved us so much that he gave his own Son to die in our stead. And now he says that he is ready to forgive, if we will repent, and believe in his Son who has suffered and died to save us. And ought we not to love so kind a Savior?

You cannot expect at present precisely and fully to understand every thing connected with the sufferings and death of Christ, and the moral effect they produce. In fact, it is intimated in the Bible, that even the angels in heaven find this subject one capable of tasking all their powers.[25] You can understand, however, that he suffered and died, that you might be forgiven. It would not be safe in any government to forgive sin merely on the penitence of the sinner. Civil government cannot do this safely; a family government cannot do it safely. It is often the case, when a man is condemned to death for a crime he has committed, that his dearest friends, sometimes his wife and children, make the most affecting appeals to the chief magistrate of the state, to grant him pardon. But it will not do. The governor, if he knows his duty, will be firm, however painful it may be, in allowing the law to take its course; for he has to consider not merely the wishes of the unhappy criminal and his friends, but the safety and happiness of the whole community.

And so the governor of the universe must consider, not merely his own benevolent feelings towards the sinner, but the safety and the holiness of all his creatures; and he could not have forgiven our sins, unless he had planned a way by which we might *safely* be forgiven. This way he

---

[24] Isaiah 53:5.
[25] 1 Peter 1:12.

did devise, to sustain law and protect holiness, and yet to let us go free from the punishment due to our sins. Jesus died for us. He bore our sins. By his stripes we are healed. And shall we not be grateful?

It is thus that God has provided a way for our escape from the penalty of his law. You have read, "God so loved the world, we that he gave his only begotten Son, that whosoever believeth in him should not perish, but have everlasting life."[26] Was it not kind in God to give his Son to suffer, that we might be saved from punishment? God has plainly given his law. And he has said, 'the soul that sinneth, it shall die.' And he has said that his word is so sacred, that, though heaven and earth should pass away, his word shall not pass away.[27] We have all broken God's law, and deserve the punishment it threatens. But our indulgent Father in heaven is looking upon us in loving kindness and in tender mercy. He pities us, and he has given his own Son to bear the punishment which we deserve. Oh, was there ever proof of greater love?

And how ardently should we love that Savior, who is nearer and dearer than a brother, who has left heaven and all its joys, and come to the world, and suffered and died, that we might be happy! God expects that we shall love him; that we shall receive him as our Savior, and whenever we do wrong, that we shall ask forgiveness for his sake. And when a child thinks of the sorrows which his sins have caused the Savior, it does appear to me that he must love that Savior with the most ardent affection.

It was the law of a certain town that the boys should not slide down hill in the streets during the snowy season. If any were found doing so, they were to be fined, and if the money was not paid, they were to be sent to jail.

---

[26] John 3:16.
[27] Cf. Matthew 24:35; Mark 13:31; Luke 21:33.

Now, a certain boy, the son of a poor man, broke the law, and was taken up by an officer. They carried him into court, the fact was fully proved against him, and he was sentenced to pay the fine. He had no money, and his father, who stood by, was poor, and found it hard work to supply the wants of the family. The money must be paid, however, or the poor boy must go to jail. The father thought that he could earn it in the evenings, and he promised, accordingly, to pay the money if they would let his son go.

Evening after evening, then, he went out to his work, while the boy was allowed to remain by the comfortable fire, at home. After a while the money was earned and paid, and then the boy felt relieved and free.

Now, suppose this boy, instead of being grateful to the father, who had suffered for him, should treat him with coldness and unkindness. Suppose he should continually do things to give him pain, and always be reluctant to do the slightest thing to oblige him. Who would not despise so ungrateful a boy?

And do you think that that child who will grieve the Savior with continued sin, who will not love him, who will not try to obey him, can have one spark of noble, of generous feeling in his bosom? Would any person, of real magnanimity, disregard a friend who had done so much as the Savior has done for us? God requires of us, that while we feel penitent for our sins, we should feel grateful to that Savior who has redeemed us by his blood. And when Jesus Christ says, "Come unto me, all ye that labor and are heavy-laden, and I will give you rest,"[28] this is what he means. We must love Christ. We must regard him as the friend who has, by his own sufferings, saved us from the

---

[28] Matthew 11:28.

penalty of God's law. And it is dishonorable and base to refuse to love him, and to do every thing in your power to please him.

This kind Savior is now looking upon you with affection. He has gone to heaven to prepare a place for you, and there he wishes to receive you, and to make you happy for ever. His eye is upon your heart every day, and every hour. He never forgets you. Wherever you go, he follows you. He shields you from harm. He supplies all your wants. He surrounds you with blessings. And now, all that he asks for all these favors is your love; not that you may do good to him, but that he may do still more good to you. He wishes to take you, holy and happy, to the green pastures and the still waters of heaven. Can any child refuse to love this Savior? Oh, go to him at once, and pray that he will receive you, and write your name among the number of his friends. Then will he soon receive you to his own blissful abode.

> "Fair distant land! could mortal eyes
>   But half its charms explore,
> How would our spirits long to rise,
>   And dwell on earth no more!
>
> No cloud those distant regions know,
>   Realms ever bright and fair!
> For sin, the source of mortal woe,
>   Can never enter there."

Every child who reads this book probably knows, that, unless he is penitent for sin, and trusts in the Savior, he must for ever be banished from the presence of God. But a person cannot be penitent and grateful who does not endeavor in all things to be obedient. You must try at all times of the day, and in all the duties of the day, to be faithful, that you may please God. It is not a little thing to be a Christian. It is not enough that you at times pray earnestly and feel deeply. You must be mild, and forbearing, and affectionate, and obedient. Do you think that child can be a Christian, who will, by ingratitude, make his parents unhappy? There is, perhaps, nothing which is more pleasing to God than to see a child who is affectionate and obedient to his parents. This is one of the most important Christian duties. And if ever you see a child who professes to be a Christian child, and who yet is guilty of ingratitude and of disobedience, you may be assured that those professions are insincere. If you would have a home in heaven, you must be obedient while in your home on earth. If you would have the favor and the affection of your heavenly Father, you must merit the affection and the gratitude of your earthly parents. God has most explicitly commanded that you should honor your father and your mother. If you sin in this respect, it is positive proof that the displeasure of God rests upon you.

Sincere love to God will make a child not only more amiable in general character, but also more industrious. You are, perhaps, at school, and, not feeling very much like study, idle away the afternoon. Now, God's eye is upon you all the time. He sees every moment which is wasted. And the sin of that idle afternoon you must render an account for, at his bar. Do you suppose that a person can be a Christian, and yet be neglecting time, and living in idleness? Even for every idle word that men shall speak they must give an account in the Day of Judgment. If you do not improve your time when young, you can neither be useful, nor respected, nor happy. The consequences of this idleness will follow you through life. With all sin God has connected sorrow. The following account of George Jones will show how intimately God has connected with indolence both sorrow and disgrace.

THE CONSEQUENCES OF IDLENESS

Many young persons seem to think it is not of much consequence if they do not improve their time well when in youth, for they can make it up by diligence when they are older. They think it is disgraceful for *men* and *women* to be idle, but that there can be no harm for persons who are *young* to spend their time in any manner they please.

George Jones thought so. He was twelve years old. He went to an academy to prepare to enter college. His father was at great expense in obtaining books for him, clothing him, and paying his tuition. But George was idle. The preceptor[29] of the academy would often tell him that if he did not study diligently when young, he would never succeed well. But George thought of nothing but present pleasure. Often would he go to school without having made any preparation for his morning lesson; and, when called to recite with his class, he would stammer and make such blunders, that the rest of his class could not help laughing at him. He was one of the poorest students in school, because he was one of the idlest.

When recess came, and all the boys ran out of the academy, upon the playground, idle George would come moping along. Instead of studying diligently while in school, he was indolent and half asleep. When the proper time for play came, he had no relish for it. I recollect very well that, when *tossing up*[30] for a game of ball, we used to choose every body on the playground before we chose George. And if there were enough to play without him, we used to leave him out. Thus was he unhappy in school and

---

[29] One who gives commands, or makes rules; specifically, the master or principal of a school; a teacher; an instructor.

[30] Choosing sides by means of flipping a coin.

out of school. There is nothing which makes a person enjoy play so well as to study hard. When recess was over, and the rest of the boys returned fresh and vigorous to their studies, George might be seen lagging and moping along to his seat. Sometimes he would be asleep in school, sometimes he would pass his time in catching flies and penning them up in little holes, which he cut in his seat. And sometimes, when the preceptor's back was turned, he would throw a paper ball across the room. When the class was called up to recite, George would come drowsily along, looking as wretched and ashamed as though he were going to be whipped. The rest of the class stepped up to the recitation with promptness, and appeared happy and contented. When it came George's turn to recite, he would be so long, and make such blunders, that all most heartily wished him out of the class.

At last George went with his class to enter college. Though he passed a very poor examination, he was admitted with the rest, for those who examined him thought it was possible, that the reason why he did not answer the questions better was that he was frightened. Now came hard times for poor George. In college there is not much mercy shown to bad students; and George had neglected his studies so long that he could not now keep up with his class, let him try ever so hard.

He could without much difficulty get along in the academy, where there were only two or three boys of his own class to laugh at him. But now he had to go into a large recitation room, filled with students from all parts of the country. In the presence of all these he must rise and recite to the professor. Poor fellow! He paid dear for his idleness. You would have pitied him, if you could have seen him trembling in his seat, every moment expecting to be called upon to recite. And when he was called upon, he would stand up and take what the class called a *dead set;* that is, he could not recite at all. Sometimes he would make such ludicrous blunders that the whole class would burst into a laugh. Such are the applauses idleness gets. He was wretched, of course. He had been idle so long, that he hardly knew how to apply his mind to study. All the good students avoided him; they were ashamed to be seen in his company. He became discouraged, and gradually grew into a degenerate.

The government of the college soon was compelled to suspend him. He returned in a few months, but did no better; and his father was then advised to take him from college. He left college, despised by every one. A few months ago I met him in New York, a poor wanderer, without money or friends. Such are the wages of idleness. I hope every reader will from this history take warning, and "stamp improvement on the wings of time."

This story of George Jones, which is a true one, shows how sinful and ruinous it is to be idle. Every child who would be a Christian, and have a home in heaven, must guard against this sin. But as I have given you one story, which shows the sad effects of indolence, I will now present you with another, more pleasing, which shows the rewards of industry.

THE ADVANTAGES OF INDUSTRY

I gave you the history of George Jones, an idle boy, and showed you the consequences of his idleness. I shall now give you the history of Charles Bullard, a classmate of George. Charles was about the same age with George, and did not possess naturally superior talents. Indeed, I doubt whether he was equal to him, in natural powers of mind. But Charles was a hard working student. When quite young, he was always careful to be diligent in school. Sometimes, when there was a *very hard* lesson, instead of going out in the recess to play, he would stay in to study. He had resolved that his first object should be to get his lesson well, and then he could play with a good conscience. He loved play as well as any body, and was one of the best players on the ground; I hardly ever saw any body catch a ball better than he could. When playing any game every one was glad to get Charles on his side. I have said that Charles would sometimes stay in at recess. This, however, was very seldom; it was only when the lesson was very hard indeed. Generally he was among the first upon the playground, and he was also among the first to go into school, when called in. Hard study gave him a relish for play, and play again gave him a relish for hard study; so he was happy both in school and out. The preceptor could not help liking him, for he always had his lessons well committed, and never gave him any trouble.

When he went to enter college, the preceptor gave him a good recommendation. He was able to answer all the questions which were put to him when he was examined. He had studied so well when he was in the academy, and was so thoroughly prepared for college, that he found it very easy to keep up with his class, and had much time for reading interesting books. But he would always first get his lesson well, before he did any thing else, and would review it just before recitation. When called upon to recite, he rose tranquil and happy, and very seldom made any mistake. The government of the college had a high opinion of him, and he was respected by all the students.

There was in the college a society made up of all of the best students. Charles was chosen a member of that society. It was the custom to choose some one of the society to deliver a public address every year. This honor was conferred on Charles; and he had studied so diligently, and read so much, that he delivered an address, which was very interesting to all who heard it. At last he *graduated*, as it is called; that is, he finished his collegiate course, and received his degree. It was known by all that he was a good scholar, and by all he was respected. His father and mother, brothers and sisters, came on commencement day, to hear him speak. They all felt gratified and loved Charles more than ever. Many situations of usefulness and profit were opened to him, for Charles was now a man, intelligent, and universally respected. He is now a useful and a happy man. He has a cheerful home, and is esteemed by all who know him.

Such are the rewards of industry. How strange is it that any persons should be willing to live in idleness, when it will certainly make them unhappy! The idle boy is almost invariably poor and miserable; the industrious boy is universally happy and prosperous.

But perhaps some child who reads this, asks, "Does God notice little children in school?" He certainly does. And if you are not diligent in the improvement of your time, it is one of the surest of evidences that your heart is not right with God. You are placed in this world to improve your time. In youth you must be preparing for future usefulness. And if you do not improve the advantages you enjoy, you sin against your Maker.

"With books, or work, or healthful play,
  Let your first years be past,
That you may give, for every day,
  Some good account at last."

One of the petitions in the Lord's Prayer is, "forgive us our debts as we forgive our debtors."[31] We do thus pray that God will exercise the same kind of forgiveness towards us, which we exercise towards others. Consequently, if we are unforgiving or revengeful, we pray that God will treat us in the same way when we appear before him in judgment. Thus God teaches the necessity of cultivating a forbearing and a forgiving spirit. We must do this or we cannot be Christians. When I was a boy, there was another little boy who went to the same school with me, who was a professed Christian. He seemed to love the Savior, and to try in all things to abstain from sin. Some of the bad boys were in the habit of ridiculing him, and of doing every thing they could to tease him, because he would not join with them in mischief. Near the schoolhouse there was a small orchard; and the students would, without the permission of the owner, take the apples. One day a group of boys were going into the orchard for fruit, and called upon this pious boy to accompany them.

"Come, Henry," said one of them to him, "let us go and get some apples."

"The apples are not ours," he fearlessly replied, "and I do not think it right to steal."

"You are a coward and afraid to go," the other replied.

"I am afraid," said Henry, "to do wrong, and you ought to be; but I am not afraid to do right."

This wicked boy was exceedingly irritated at this rebuke, and called Henry all manner of names, and endeavored to hold him up to the ridicule of the whole school.

---

[31] Matthew 6:12.

Henry bore it very patiently, though it was hard to be endured, for the boy who ridiculed him had a great deal of influence and talent.

Some days after this the boys were going fishing. Henry had a beautiful fishing-rod, which his father had bought for him.

George—for by that name I shall call the boy who abused Henry—was very desirous of borrowing this fishing-rod, and yet was ashamed to ask for it. At last, however, he summoned courage, and called out to Henry upon the playground—

"Henry, will you lend me your rod to go fishing?"

"O yes," said Henry; "if you will go home with me, I will get it for you now."

Poor George felt ashamed enough for what he had done. But he went home with Henry to get the rod.

They went up into the barn together, and when Henry had taken his fishing-tackle from the place in which he kept it, he said to George, "I have a new line in the house, which father bought me the other day; you may have that too, if you want it." George could hardly hold up his head, he felt so ashamed. However, Henry went and got the new line, and placed it upon the rod, and gave them into George's hand.

A few days after this, George told me about it. "Why," said he, "I never felt so ashamed in my life. And one thing is certain; I will never call Henry names again."

Now, who does not admire the conduct of Henry in this affair? This forgiving spirit is what God requires. The child, who would be the friend of God, must possess this spirit. You must always be ready to forgive. You must never indulge in the feelings of revenge. You must never desire to injure another, how much soever you may feel that others have injured you. The spirit of the Christian is a forgiving spirit.

God also requires of his friends, that they shall ever be doing good, as they have opportunity. The Christian child will do all in his power to make those happy who are about him. He will disregard himself that he may promote the happiness of others. He will be obliging to all.

This world is not your home. You are to remain here but a few years, and then go to that home of joy or woe, which you never, never will leave. God expects you to be useful here. "How can I do any good?" do you say? Why, in many ways. You can make your parents happy; that is doing good. You can make your brothers and sisters happy; that is doing good. You can try to make your brothers and sisters more obedient to their parents; that is doing good. You can set a good example at school; that is doing good. If you see your companions doing any thing that is wrong, you can try to dissuade them. You can speak to your bosom friend, upon the Savior's goodness, and endeavor to excite in his heart the feelings which are in yours. Thus you may be exerting a good influence upon all around you. Your life will not be spent in vain. God will smile upon you, and give joy in a dying hour.

Some children appear to think that if they are Christians, they cannot be as happy as they may be if they are not Christians. They think that to love God, and to pray, and to do their duty, is gloomy work. But God tells us that none can be happy but those who love him. And every one who has repented of sin, and loves the Savior, says that there is more happiness in this mode of life than in any other. We may indeed be happy a little while without piety. But misfortunes and sorrows will come. Your hopes of pleasure will be disappointed. You will be called to weep; to suffer pain; to die. And there is nothing but religion which can give you a happy life and a peaceful death. It is that you may be happy, not unhappy, that God wishes you to be a Christian.

It is true that at times it requires a very great struggle to take a decided stand as a Christian. The proud heart is reluctant to yield. The worldly spirit clings to worldly pleasure. It requires bravery and resolution to meet the obstacles which will be thrown in your way. You may be opposed. You may be ridiculed. But, notwithstanding all this, the only way to ensure happiness is to love and serve your Maker. Many children know that they ought to love God, and wish that they had resolution to do their duty. But they are afraid of the ridicule of their companions. Henry, who would not rob the orchard, was a brave boy. He knew that they would laugh at him. But what did he care? He meant to do his duty without being frightened if others did laugh. And the consciousness of doing his duty afforded him much greater enjoyment than he could possibly have received from eating the stolen fruit. Others of the boys went and robbed the orchard, because they had not courage to refuse to do as their companions did. They knew it was wrong, but they were afraid of being laughed at. But which is the most easy to be borne, the ridicule of the wicked, or a condemning conscience, and the displeasure of God? It is so with all the duties of the Christian. If you will conscientiously do that which God approves, he will give you peace of mind, and prepare you for eternal joy.

One of the most eminent and useful of the English clergymen was led, when a child, by the following interesting circumstance, to surrender himself to the Savior. When a little boy, he was, like other children, playful and thoughtless. He thought, perhaps, that he would wait until he was old, before he became a Christian.

His father was a pious man, and frequently conversed with him about heaven, and urged him to prepare to die.

On the evening of his birthday, when he was ten years of age, his father took him affectionately by the hand, and reminding him of the scenes through which he had already passed, urged him to commence that evening a life of piety. He told him of the love of Jesus. He told him of the danger of delay. And he showed him that he must perish for ever unless he speedily trusted in the Savior, and gave his life to his service. As this child thought of a dying hour, and of a Savior's love, his heart was full of feeling, and the tears gushed into his eyes. He felt that it was time for him to choose whether he would live for God or for the world. He resolved that he would no longer delay.

His father and mother then retired to their chamber to pray for their child, and this child also went to his chamber to pray for himself. Sincerely he gave himself to the Savior. Earnestly he implored forgiveness, and most fervently entreated God to aid him to keep his resolutions and to refrain from sin. And do you think that child was not happy, as, in the silence of his chamber, he surrendered himself to God? It was undoubtedly the hour of the purest enjoyment he ever had experienced. Angels looked with joy upon that evening scene, and hovered with delight and love around that penitent child. The prayers of the parent and the child ascended as grateful incense to the throne, and were accepted. And from that affecting hour, this little boy went on in the path which leads to usefulness, and peace, and heaven. He spent his life in doing good. A short time ago, he died a veteran soldier of the cross, and is now undoubtedly amid the glories of heaven, surrounded by hundreds, who have been, by his instrumentality, led to those green fields and loved mansions. Oh, what a rapturous meeting must that have been, when the parents of this child pressed forward from the angel throng, to welcome him, as, with triumphant wing, he entered heaven! And, oh, how happy must they now be, in that home of songs and everlasting joy!

It is thus that piety promotes our enjoyment. It promotes our happiness at all times. It takes away the fear of death, and deprives every sorrow of half its bitterness. Death is the gloomiest thought that can enter the minds of those who are not Christians. But the pious child can be happy even when dying. I was once called to see a boy who was very dangerously sick, and expected soon to die. I expected to have found him sorrowful. But, instead of that, a happy smile was on his countenance, which showed that joy was in his heart. He sat in bed, leaning upon his pillow, with a hymn book in his hand, which he was reading. His cheeks were thin and pale, from his long sickness, while, at the same time, he appeared contented and happy. After conversing with him a little while, I said,

"Do you think you shall ever get well again?"

"No, sir," he cheerfully replied, "the doctor says I may perhaps live a few weeks, but that he should not be surprised if I should die at any time."

"Are you willing to die?" I said.

"O yes, sir," he answered; "sometimes I feel sad about leaving father and mother. But then I think I shall be free from sin in heaven, and shall be with the Savior. And I hope that father and mother will soon come to heaven, and I shall be with them then. I am sometimes afraid that I am too impatient to go."

"What makes you think," I asked, "that you are prepared to die?"

He hesitated for a moment, and then said, "Because Jesus Christ has said, 'Whosoever cometh to me I will in no wise cast out.'[32] I do think that I love the Savior, and I wish to go to him, and to be made holy."

While talking with him, I heard some boys laughing and playing under the window. But this sick boy looked up to me, and said, "Oh, how much more happy am I now, than I used to be when well and out at play, not thinking of God or heaven! There is not a boy in the street as happy as I."

This little boy had for some time been endeavoring to do his duty as a Christian. His conduct showed that he loved the Savior. And when sickness came, and death was near, he was happy. But, oh, how sad must that child feel, who is dying in unconfessed and unforgiven sin! We all must certainly soon die, and there is nothing to make us happy in death but piety.

But when the Christian child goes to heaven, how happy must he be! He rises above the clouds, and the blue sky, and the twinkling stars, till he enters the home of God and the angels. There he becomes like an angel himself. God gives him a body of perfect beauty, and perhaps furnishes him with wings, with which he can fly from world to world. God is his approving Father. Angels are his beloved friends. You often, in a clear evening, look up upon the distant stars, and wonder who inhabits them. You think, if you had the wings of an eagle, you would love to fly up there, and make a visit. Now, it is not improbable that the Christian, in heaven, can pass from star to star, as you can go from house to house in your own neighborhood. The very thought is enrapturing. If every hour of our lives were spent in sorrow, it would be nothing, compared with the joys which God has promised his friends at his right hand. When we think of the green

---

[32] John 6:37.

pastures of heaven; of the still waters of that happy world; when we think of mingling with the angels in their flight; of uniting our voices with theirs in songs of praise; of gazing upon all the glories and sharing all the rapture of the heavenly world—O, how tame do the joys of earth appear!

Some children, however, think that they can put off becoming Christians till a dying hour, and then repent and be saved. Even if you could do this, it would be at the loss of much usefulness and much happiness. But the fact is, you are never certain of a moment of life. You are little aware of the dangers to which you are continually exposed.

"The rising morning can't assure,
  That we shall spend the day;
For death stands ready at the door,
  To snatch our lives away."

We are reminded of the uncertainty of life, by the accidents which are every day occurring. Often, when we least suspect it, we are in the most imminent hazard of our lives. When I was a boy, I one day went hunting. I was to call for another boy, who lived at a little distance from my father's. Having loaded my gun with a heavy charge of pigeon-shot, and put in a new flint, which would strike out a brilliant shower of sparks, I carefully primed the gun, and set out upon my expedition. When arrived at the house of the boy who was to go with me, I leaned the gun against the side of the house, and waited a few moments for him to get ready. About a rod[33] from the door, where I was waiting, there was another house. A little girl stood upon the window-seat, looking out of the window. Another boy

---

[33] (British) a linear measure of 16.5 feet.

came along, and, taking up the gun, not knowing that it was loaded and primed, took deliberate aim at the face of the girl, and pulled the trigger. But God, in mercy, caused the gun to misfire. Had it gone off, the girl's face would have been blown all to pieces. I never can think of the danger she was in, even now, without trembling. The girl did not see the boy take aim at her, and does not now know how narrow her escape from death was. She little supposed that, when standing in perfect health by the window in her own father's house, she was in danger of dropping down dead upon the floor. We are all continually exposed to such dangers, and when we least suspect it, may be in the greatest peril. Is it not, then, folly to delay preparation for death? You may die within one hour. You may not have one moment of warning allowed you.

A few years ago, a little boy was riding in the stagecoach. It was a pleasant summer's day. The horses were trotting rapidly along by fields, and bridges, and orchards, and houses. The little boy stood at the coach window with a happy heart, and looked upon the green fields and pleasant dwellings; upon the poultry in the farm-yards, and the cattle upon the hills. He had not the least idea that he should die that day. But while he was looking out of the window, the iron rim of the wheel broke, and struck him upon the forehead. The poor boy lay senseless for a few days, and then died. There are a thousand ways by which life may be suddenly extinguished, and yet how seldom are they thought of by children! They almost always entirely forget the danger of early death, and postpone to a future day making their peace with God. And how little do those who read this book think that they may die suddenly! Many children, when they go to bed at night, say the prayer,

"Now I lay me down to sleep,
  I pray the Lord my soul to keep,
If I should die before I wake,
  I pray the Lord my soul to take."

I used to say this prayer, when a child, every night before I went to sleep. But I did not know then, as well as I do now, that I might die before the morning. Almost every night some children go to bed well, and before morning are dead. It is, therefore, very dangerous to delay repentance. Love the Savior immediately, and prepare to die, and it will be of but little consequence when you die, for you will go to heaven and be happy for ever.

But we must not forget that a most terrible doom awaits those who will not serve their Maker. It matters not how much we may be beloved by our friends; how amiable may be our feelings. This alone will not save us. We must repent of sin, and love the Savior, who has suffered for us. We must pass our lives in usefulness and prayer, or, when the Day of Judgment comes, we shall hear the sentence, "Depart from me, for I know you not."[34] It is indeed a fearful thing to refuse affection and obedience to our Father in heaven. He will receive none into his happy family above, but those who love him. He will have no angry, disagreeable spirits there. He will receive none but the penitent, and the humble, and the grateful, to that pure and peaceful home.

Who does not wish to go to heaven? O, then, now begin to do your duty, and earnestly pray that God will forgive your sins, and give you a heart to love and obey him.

---

[34] Paraphrase of Matthew 7:23.

Chapter Seven

Traits of Character

Every child must observe how much more happy and beloved some children appear to be than others. There are some children you always love to be with. They are happy themselves, and they make you happy. There are others whose society you always avoid. The very expression of their countenances produces unpleasant feelings. They seem to have no friends.

No person can be happy without friends. The heart is formed for love, and cannot be happy without the opportunity of giving and receiving affection.

> "It's not in titles, nor in rank,
> It's not in wealth like London bank,
>   To make us truly blest.
> If happiness have not her seat
>   And centre in the breast,
> We may be wise, or rich, or great,
>   But never can be blest."

But you cannot receive affection, unless you will also give. You cannot find others to love you, unless you will also love them. Love is only to be obtained by giving

113

love in return. Hence the importance of cultivating a cheerful and obliging disposition. You cannot be happy without it. I have sometimes heard a girl say, "I know that I am very unpopular at school." Now, this is simply saying that she is very disobliging and unamiable in her disposition. If your companions do not love you, it is usually your own fault. They cannot help loving you if you will be kind and friendly. If you are not loved, it is good evidence that you do not deserve to be loved. It is true that a sense of duty may at times render it necessary for you to do that which is displeasing to your companions. But if it is seen that you have a noble spirit; that you are above selfishness; that you are willing to make sacrifices of your own personal convenience to promote the happiness of your associates, you will never be in want of friends. You must not regard it as your misfortune that others do not love you, but your own fault. It is not beauty; it is not wealth that will give you friends. Your heart must glow with kindness if you would attract to yourself the esteem and affection of those by whom you are surrounded.

You are little aware how much the happiness of your whole life depends upon your cultivating an affectionate and obliging disposition. If you will adopt the resolution that you will confer favors whenever you have an opportunity, you will certainly be surrounded by ardent friends. Begin upon this principle in childhood, and act upon it through life, and you will make yourself happy, and promote the happiness of all within your influence.

You go to school in a cold winter morning. A bright fire is blazing upon the hearth, surrounded with boys struggling to get near it to warm themselves. After you get slightly warmed, another schoolmate comes in suffering with the cold.

114

"Here, James," you pleasantly call out to him, "I am most warm; you may have my place."

As you slip to one side to allow him to take your place at the fire, will he not feel that you are kind? The boy with the worst disposition in the world cannot help admiring such generosity. And even though he be so ungrateful as to be unwilling to return the favor, you may depend upon it that he will be your friend, as far as he is capable of friendship. If you will habitually act upon this principle, you will never want for friends.

Suppose some day you are out with your companions playing ball. After you have been playing for some time, another boy comes along. He cannot be chosen upon either side; for there is no one to match him.

"Henry," you say, "you may take my place a little while, and I will rest."

You throw yourself down upon the grass, while Henry, fresh and vigorous, takes your bat, and engages in the game. He knows that you gave up to oblige him. And how can he help liking you for it? The fact is that neither man nor child can cultivate such a spirit of generosity and kindness, without attracting affection and esteem. Look and see who of your companions have the most friends, and you will find that they are those who have this noble spirit; who are willing to deny themselves, that they may make their associates happy. This is not peculiar to childhood, but is the same in all periods of life. There is but one way to make friends, and that is by being friendly to others.

Perhaps some child who reads this, feels conscious of being disliked, and yet desires to have the affection of companions. You ask me what you shall do. I will tell you what. I will give you an infallible recipe. *Do all in your power to make others happy. Be willing to make sacrifices of your own convenience that you may promote the happiness of others.* This is the way to make friends, and the only way. When you are playing with your brothers and sisters at home, be always ready to give them more than their share of privileges. Manifest an obliging disposition, and they cannot but regard you with affection. In all your intercourse with others, at home or abroad, let these feelings influence you, and you will receive the rich reward of devoted friends.

The very exercise of these feelings brings enjoyment. The benevolent man is a cheerful man. His family is happy. His home is the abode of the purest earthly joy. These feelings are worth cultivating, for they bring with them their own reward. Benevolence is the spirit of heaven. Selfishness is the spirit of the fiend.

> "The heart benevolent and kind
> The most resembles God."

But persons of ardent dispositions often find it exceedingly difficult to deny themselves. Some little occurrence irritates them, and they speak hastily and angrily. Offended with a companion, they will do things to give pain, instead of pleasure. You must have your temper under control if you would exercise a friendly disposition. A bad temper is an infirmity, which, if not restrained, will be continually growing worse and worse. There was a man, a few years ago, tried for murder. When a boy, he gave vent to his passions. The least opposition would rouse his anger, and he made no efforts to subdue himself. He had no one who could love him. If he was playing with others, he would every moment be getting irritated. As he grew older, his passions increased, and he became so ill-natured that every one avoided him. One day, as he was talking with another man, he became so enraged at some little provocation, that he seized a club, and with one blow laid the man lifeless at his feet. He was seized and imprisoned. But, while in prison, the fury of a malignant and ungoverned spirit increased to such a degree that he became a maniac. The very fires of the world of woe were burning in his heart. Loaded with chains, and caged in a dark dungeon, he was doomed to pass the miserable remnant of his guilty life, the victim of his own ungovernable passion.

This is a very unusual case. But nothing is more common than for a child to destroy his own peace, and to make his brothers and sisters continually unhappy by indulging in a peevish and irritable spirit. Nothing is more common than for a child to cherish this disposition until he becomes a man, and then, by his peevishness and fault-finding, he destroys the happiness of all who are near him. His home is the scene of discord. His family is made wretched and miserable.

An amiable disposition makes its possessor happy. And if you would have such a disposition, you must learn to control yourself. If others injure you, then follow the gospel rule, and do them good in return. If they revile you, speak kindly to them. It is far better to suffer injury than to inflict injury. If you will endeavor in childhood in this way to control your passions, to be always mild, and forbearing, and forgiving, you will disarm opposition, and, in many cases, convert enemies to friends. You will be beloved by those around you, and when you have a home of your own, your cheerful and obliging spirit will make it a happy home.

One thing you may be sure of. There can be no real happiness when there is not an amiable disposition. You cannot more surely make yourself wretched, than by indulging in an irritable spirit. Love is the feeling which fills every angel's bosom; and it is the feeling which should fill every human heart. It is love which will raise us to the angel's throne. It is malice which will sink us to the demon's dungeon. I hope that every child who reads this, will be persuaded, by these remarks, immediately to commence the government of his temper. Resolve that you never will be angry. If your brother or your sister does any thing which has a tendency to provoke you, restrain your feelings, and speak mildly and softly. Let no provocation draw from you an angry or an unkind word. If you will commence in this way, and persevere, you will soon get that control over yourself that will contribute greatly to your happiness. Your friends will increase, and you will be prepared for far more extensive usefulness in the world.

And is there not something noble in being able to be always calm and pleasant? I once saw two men conversing in the streets. One became very unreasonably enraged with the other. In the fury of his anger, he appeared like a madman. He addressed the other in language the most abusive and insulting. The gentleman, whom he thus abused, with a pleasant countenance and a calm voice, said to him, "Now, my friend, you will be sorry for all this when your passion is over. This language does me no harm, and can do you no good."

Now is it not really magnanimous to have such a spirit? Every person who witnessed this interview despised the angry man, and respected the one who was so calm and self-possessed.

Humility is another very important trait of character, which should be cultivated in early life. What can be more disgusting than the ridiculous airs[35] of a vain

---

[35] Affected manners intended to impress others; "don't put on airs with me"

child? Sometimes you will see a foolish girl tossing her head about, and walking with a mincing step,[36] which shows you at once that she is excessively vain. She thinks that others are admiring her ridiculous airs, when the fact is; they are laughing at her, and despising her. Every one speaks of her as a very simple, vain girl. Vanity is a sure sign of weakness of mind; and if you indulge in so contemptible a passion, you will surely be the subject of ridicule and contempt. A young lady was once passing an afternoon at the house of a friend. As she, with one or two gentlemen and ladies, was walking in the garden, she began to make a display of her imaginary learning. She would look at a flower, and with great self-sufficiency talk of its botanical characteristics. She thought that the company were all marveling at the extent of her knowledge, when they were all laughing at her, as a self-conceited girl who had not sense enough to keep herself from appearing ridiculous. The gentlemen were winking at one another, and slyly laughing as she uttered one learned word after another, with an affected air of familiarity with scientific terms. During the walk, she took occasion to drag in all the little she knew, and at one time ventured to quote a little Latin for their edification. Poor simpleton! She thought she had produced quite an impression upon their minds. And, in truth, she had. She had fixed indelibly the impression that she was an insufferably weak and self-conceited girl. She made herself the laughing-stock of the whole company. The moment she was gone, there was one general burst of laughter. And not one of those gentlemen or ladies could ever think of that vain girl afterwards, without emotions of contempt.

---

[36] Characterized by primness or affected nicety.

This is the invariable effect of vanity. You cannot so disguise it, but that it will be detected, and cover you with disgrace. There is no foible more common than this, and there is none more supremely ridiculous.

One boy happens to have rich parents, and he acts as though he supposed that there was some virtue in his father's money which pertained to him. He goes to school and struts about, as though he were lord of the playground. Now, every body who sees this, says, it is a proof that the boy has not much of a mind. He is a simple boy. If he had good sense he would perceive that others of his playmates, in many qualities, surpassed him, and that it became him to be humble and unostentatious. The mind that is truly great is humble.

We are all disgusted with vanity wherever it appears. Go into a school-room, and look around upon the appearance of the various pupils assembled there. You will perhaps see one girl, with head tossed upon one shoulder, and with a simpering countenance, trying to look pretty. You speak to her. Instead of receiving a plain, kind, honest answer, she replies with voice and language and attitude full of embellishment. She thinks she is exciting your admiration. But, on the contrary, she is exciting disgust and loathing.

You see another girl, whose frank and open countenance proclaims a sincere and honest heart. All her movements are natural. She manifests no desire to attract attention. The idea of her own superiority seems not to enter her mind. As, in the recess, she walks about the school-room, you can detect no airs of self-conceit. She is pleasant to all her associates. You ask her some question. She answers you with modesty and unpretentiousness. Now, this girl, without any effort to attract admiration, is beloved and admired. Every one sees at once that she is a girl of good sense. She knows too much to be vain. She will never want for friends. This is the kind of character which insures usefulness and happiness.

A little girl who had rich parents, and was handsome in personal appearance, was very vain of her beauty and of her father's wealth. She disgusted all her school-mates by her conceit. And though she seemed to think that every one ought to admire her, she was beloved by none. She at last left school, a vain, disgusting girl. A young man, who was so simple as to fall in love with this piece of pride and affectation, at length married her. For a few years the property which she received of her father supported them. But soon her father died, and her husband grew into a degenerate, and before long their property was all squandered. She had no friends to whom she could look for assistance, and they were every month sinking deeper and deeper in poverty. Her husband at last became a perfect sot,[37] and staggered through the streets in the lowest state of degradation. She was left with one or two small children, and without any means of support. In a most miserable hovel, this poor woman was compelled to take up her residence. By this time, her pride had experienced a fall. She no longer exhibited the airs of a vain girl, but was an afflicted and helpless woman. The sorrow and disgrace into which she was plunged by the intemperance of her husband, preyed so deeply upon her feelings as to destroy her health, and in this condition she was carried to the poor-house. There she lingered out the few last years of her sad earthly existence. What a termination of life for a vain and haughty girl! And what a lesson is this to all, to be humble and unassuming! You may be in health today, and in sickness tomorrow. This

---

[37] A person stupefied by excessive drinking; an habitual drunkard.

year you may be rich, and have need of nothing, and the next year you may be in the most abject poverty. Your early home may be one of luxury and elegance, and in your dying hour you may be in the poor-house, without a friend to watch at your bedside. Is it not, then, the height of folly to indulge in vanity?

If any child will look around upon his own companions, he will see that those are most beloved and respected, who have no disposition to claim superiority over their associates. How pleasant is it to be in company with those who are conciliating and unassuming! But how much is every one disgusted with the presence of those who assume airs of importance, and are continually saying, by their conduct, that they think themselves deserving particular attention! No one regrets to see such self-conceit humbled. When such persons meet with misfortune, no one appears to regret it, no one sympathizes with them.

You must guard against this contemptible vice, if you would be useful, or respected, or happy. If you would avoid exciting disgust, avoid vanity. If you do not wish to be the laughing-stock of all your acquaintances, do not let them detect in you consequential airs. If you would not be an object of hatred and disgust, beware how you indulge feelings of fancied superiority. Be plain, and sincere, and honest-hearted. Disgrace not yourself by affectation and pride. Let all your words and all your actions show that you think no more highly of yourself than you ought to think. Then will others love you. They will rejoice at your prosperity. And they will be glad to see you rising in the world, in usefulness and esteem.

Moral courage is a trait of character of the utmost importance to be possessed. A man was once challenged to fight a duel. As he thought of his own condition, if he should kill his adversary, and of his widowed wife and orphan children, if he should be shot himself—as he thought of his appearance before the bar of God to answer for the atrocious sin, he shrunk from accepting the challenge. But when he thought of the ridicule to which he would be exposed if he declined; that others would call him a coward, and point at him the finger of scorn, he was afraid to refuse. He was such a coward that he did not dare to meet the ridicule of contemptible men. He had so little moral courage, that he had rather become a murderer, or expose himself to be shot, than boldly to disregard the opinions and the sneers of the unprincipled and base. It is this want of moral courage which very frequently leads persons to the commission of crimes.

There is nothing so hard to be borne as ridicule. It requires a bold heart to be ready to do one's duty, unmoved by the sneers of others. How often does a child do that which he knows to be wrong, because he is afraid that others will call him a coward if he does right! One cold winter's day, three boys were passing by a school-house. The oldest was a mischievous fellow, always in trouble himself, and trying to get others into trouble. The youngest, whose name was George, was a very amiable boy, who wished to do right, but was very deficient in moral courage. We will call the oldest Henry, and the other of the three James. The following dialogue passed between them.

Henry—What fun it would be to throw a snow-ball against the schoolroom door, and make the instructor and students all jump!

James—You would jump if you should. If the instructor did not catch you and whip you, he would tell your father, and you would get a whipping then, that would make you jump higher than the students, I think.

Henry—Why, we could get so far off, before the instructor could come to the door, that he could not tell who we are. Here is a snow-ball just as hard as ice, and George was as glad to throw it against that door as not.

James—Give it to him and see. He would not dare to throw it against the door.

Henry—Do you think George is a coward? You don't know him as well as I do. Here, George, take this snow-ball, and show James that you are not such a coward as he thinks you to be.

George—I am not afraid to throw it. But I do not want to. I do not see that it will do any good, or that there will be any fun in it.

James—There, I told you he would not dare to throw it.

Henry—Why, George, are you turning coward? I thought you did not fear any thing. We shall have to call you chicken-hearted. Come, save your credit, and throw it. I know you are not afraid to.

George—Well, I am not afraid to, said George. Give me the snow-ball. I am as glad to throw it as not.

Whack went the snow-ball against the door; and the boys took to their heels. Henry was laughing as heartily as he could to think what a fool he had made of George. George afterwards got a whipping for his folly, as he richly deserved. He was such a coward that he was afraid of being called a coward. He did not dare to refuse to do as Henry told him do, for fear that he would be laughed at. If he had been really a brave boy, he would have said,

"Henry, do you suppose that I am such a fool as to throw that snow-ball just because you want to have me? You may throw your own snow-balls, if you please."

Henry would perhaps have tried to laugh at him. He would have called him a coward, hoping in this way to induce him to obey his wishes. But George would have replied, "Do you think that I care for your laughing? I do not think it is right to throw a snow-ball against the schoolroom door. And I will not do that which I think to be wrong, if the whole town join with you in laughing."

This would have been real moral courage. Henry would have seen at once, that it would do no good to laugh at a boy who had so bold a heart. And you must have this fearlessness of spirit, or you will be continually involved in trouble, and will deserve and receive contempt.

I once knew a man who had so little independence, that he hardly dared express an opinion different from that of those he was with. When he was talking upon politics, he would agree with the persons with whom he happened to be conversing, no matter what their views, or what their party. He was equally fickle and undecided upon the subject of religion, differing from none, and agreeing with all. The consequence was that he had the confidence of none, and the contempt of all. He sunk into deserved disgrace in the estimation of the whole community.

You must have an opinion of your own. And you must be ready, frankly and modestly, to express it, when occasion requires, without being intimidated by fear of censure. You can neither command respect nor be useful without it.

In things which concern your own personal convenience merely, you should be as yielding as the air. But where duty is concerned, you should be as firm and as unyielding as the rock. Be ever ready to sacrifice your own comfort to promote the comfort of others. Be conciliating and obliging in all your feelings and actions. Show that you are ready to do every thing in your power to make those around you happy. Let no one have occasion to say that you are stubborn and unaccommodating.

But, on the other hand, where duty is involved, let nothing tempt you to do wrong. Be bold enough to dare to do right, whatever may be the consequences. If others laugh at your scruples, let them laugh as long as they please. And let them see that you are not to be frightened by their sneers. Your courage will often be tried. There will be occasions in which it will require a severe struggle to preserve your integrity. But ever remember that if you would do any good in the world, you must possess this moral courage. It is the want of this that leaves thousands to live in a way which their consciences reprove, and to die in despair. Unless you possess this trait of character, to some considerable degree, it can hardly be expected that you will ever become a Christian. You must learn to act for yourself, un-intimidated by the censure, and unmoved by the flattery of others.

I now bring this book to a close. If you will diligently endeavor to be influenced by its directions your usefulness and happiness will surely be promoted. Soon you will leave home, no more to return but as a visitor. The character you have acquired and the habits you have formed while at home, in all probability, will accompany you through life. You are now surrounded by all the joys of home. Affectionate parents watch over you, supplying all your wants. You have but few concerns and but few sorrows. Soon, however, you must leave parents, brothers, and sisters, and enter upon the duties and cares of life almost alone. How affecting will be the hour, when your foot steps from your father's dwelling, from your mother's care, to seek a new home among strangers! You now cannot conceive the feelings which will press upon you as your father takes your hand to bid you the parting farewell, and your mother endeavors to hide her tears, as you depart from her watchful eye, to meet the temptations and sorrows of life. Your heart will then be full. Tears will fill your eyes. Emotion will choke your voice.

You will then reflect upon all the scenes of your childhood with feelings you never had before. Every unkind word you have uttered to your parents—every unkind look you have given them will cause you the sincerest sorrow. If you have one particle of generous feeling remaining in your bosom, you will long to fall upon your knees and ask your parents' forgiveness for every pang you may have caused their hearts. The hour when you leave your home, and all its joys, will be such an hour as you never have passed before. The feelings which will then oppress your heart will remain with you for weeks and months. You will often, in the pensive hour of evening, sit down and weep, as you think of parents and home far away. Oh, how cold will seem the love of others, compared with a mother's love! How often will your thoughts fondly return to joys which have for ever fled! Again and again will you think over the years that are past. Every recollection of affection and obedience will awaken joy in your heart. Every remembrance of ingratitude will awaken repentance and remorse.

O, then, think of the time when you must bid father and mother, brothers and sisters, farewell. Think of the time when you must leave the fireside around which you have spent so many pleasant evenings, and go out into the wide world, with no other dependence than the character you have formed at home. If this character be good, if you possess amiable and obliging and generous feelings, you may soon possess a home of your own, when the joys of your childhood will in some degree be renewed. And if you will pass your days in the service of God, imitating the character of the Savior, and cherishing the feelings of penitence and love, which the Bible requires, you will soon be in that happy home which is never to be forsaken. There, are joys from which you never will be separated. There, are friends, angels in dignity and spotless in purity, in whose loved society you will find joys such as you never experienced while on earth.

When a son was leaving the roof of a pious father, to go out into the wide world to meet its temptations, and to battle with its storms, his heart was oppressed with the many emotions which were struggling there. The day had come in which he was to leave the fireside of so many enjoyments; the friends endeared to him by so many associations—so many acts of kindness. He was to bid adieu to his mother, that loved, loved benefactor, who had protected him in sickness, and rejoiced with him in health. He was to leave a father's protection, to go forth and act without an adviser, and rely upon his own unaided judgment. He was to bid farewell to brothers and sisters, no more to see them but as an occasional visitor at his paternal home. Oh, how cold and desolate did the wide world appear! How did he hesitate from launching forth to meet its tempests and its storms! But the hour had come for him to go; and he must suppress his emotions, and triumph over his reluctance. He went from room to room, looking, as for the last time, upon those scenes, to which imagination would so often recur, and where it would love to linger. The well-packed trunk was in the entryway, waiting the arrival of the stagecoach. Brothers and sisters were moving about, hardly knowing whether to smile or to cry. The father sat at the window, humming a mournful tune, as he was watching the approach of the stage which was to bear his son away to take his place far from home, in the busy crowd of a bustling world. The mother, with all the indescribable emotions of a mother's heart, was placing in a small bundle a few little comforts such as none but a mother could think of, and, with most generous resolution, endeavoring to preserve a cheerful countenance, that, as far as possible, she might preserve her son from unnecessary pain in the hour of departure.

"Here, my son," said she "is a nice pair of stockings, which will be soft and warm for your feet. I have run the heels for you,[38] for I am afraid you will not find any one who will quite fill a mother's place."

The poor boy was overflowing with emotion, and did not dare to trust his voice with an attempt to reply.

"I have put a little piece of cake here, for you may be hungry on the road, and I will put it in the top of the bundle, so that you can get it without any difficulty. And in this needle-book I have put up a few needles and some thread, for you may at times want some little stitch taken, and you will have no mother or sister to go to."

The departing son could make no reply. He could retain his emotion only by silence. At last the rumbling of the wheels of the stage was heard, and the four horses were reined up at the door. The boy endeavored, by activity, in seeing his trunk and other baggage properly placed, to gain sufficient fortitude to enable him to articulate his farewell. He, however, strove in vain. He took his mother's hand. The tear glistened for a moment in her eye, and then silently rolled down her cheek. He struggled with all his energy to say goodbye, but he could not. In unbroken silence he shook her hand, and then in

---

[38] From *The American Frugal Housewife* (1832) we read, "Run the heels of stockings faithfully; and mend thin places, as well as holes; 'a stitch in time saves nine.'"

silence received the adieus of brothers and sisters, as one after another took the hand of their departing companion. He then took the warm hand of his warm-hearted father. His father tried to smile, but it was the struggling smile of feelings which would rather have vented themselves in tears. For a moment he said not a word, but retained the hand of his son, as he accompanied him out of the door to the stage. After a moment's silence, pressing his hand, he said, "My son, you are now leaving us; you may forget your father and your mother, your brothers and your sisters, but, oh, my son, forget not your God!"

The stage door closed upon the boy. The crack of the driver's whip was heard, and the rumbling wheels bore him rapidly away from all the privileges and all the happiness of his early home. His feelings, so long restrained, now burst out, and, sinking back upon his seat, he enveloped himself in his cloak, and burst into tears.

Hour after hour the stage rolled on. Passengers entered and left; but the boy (perhaps I ought rather to call him the young man) was almost insensible to every thing that passed. He sat, in sadness and in silence, in the corner of the stage, thinking of the beloved home he had left. Memory ran back through all the years of his childhood, lingering here and there, with pain, upon an act of disobedience, and recalling an occasional word of unkindness. All his life seemed to be passing in review before him, from the first years of his conscious existence, to the hour of his departure from his home. Then would the parting words of his father ring in his ears. He had always heard the morning and evening prayer. He had always witnessed the power of religion exemplified in all the duties of life. And the undoubted sincerity of a father's language, confirmed as it had been by years of corresponding practice, produced an impression upon his mind too powerful ever to be effaced—"My son, you may forget father and mother, you may forget brothers and sisters, but, oh, my son, forget not your God." The words rung in his ears. They entered his heart. Again and again his thoughts ran back through the years he had already passed, and the reviving recollections brought fresh floods of tears. But still his thoughts ran on to his father's parting words, "forget not your God."

It was midnight before the stage stopped, to give him a little rest. He was then more than a hundred miles from home. But still his father's words were ringing in his ears. He was conducted up several flights of stairs to a chamber in a crowded hotel. After a short prayer, he threw himself upon the bed, and endeavored to obtain a little sleep. But his excited imagination ran back to the home he had left. Again he was seated by the fireside. Again he heard the soothing tones of his kind mother's voice, and sat by his father's side. In the vagaries of his dream, he again went through the scene of parting, and wept in his sleep as he bade adieu to brothers and sisters, and heard a father's parting advice, "Oh, my son, forget not your God."

But little refreshment could be derived from such sleep. And indeed he had been less than an hour upon his bed, before some one knocked at the door, and placed a lamp in his room, saying, "It is time to get up, sir: the stage is almost ready to go." He hastily rose from his bed, and after imploring a blessing upon himself, and fervently commending to God his far-distant friends, now quietly sleeping in that happy home which he had left for ever, he hastened down stairs, and soon again was rapidly borne away by the fleet horses of the mail-coach.

It was a clear autumn morning. The stars shone brightly in the sky, and the thoughts of the lonely wanderer were irresistibly carried to that home beyond the stars, and to that God whom his father had so affectingly entreated him not to forget. He succeeded, however, in getting a few moments of troubled sleep, as the stage rolled on; but his thoughts were still reverting, whether asleep or awake, to the home left far behind. Just as the sun was going down the western hills, at the close of the day, he alighted from the stage, in the village of strangers, in which he was to find his new home. Not an individual there had he ever seen before. Many a pensive evening did he pass, thinking of absent friends. Many a lonely walk did he take, while his thoughts were far away among the scenes of his childhood. And when the winter evenings came, with the cheerful blaze of the fireside, often did he think, with a sigh, of the loved and happy group encircling his father's fireside, and sharing those joys he had left for ever. But a father's parting words did not leave his mind. There they remained. And they, in connection with other events, rendered effectual by the Spirit of God, induced him to endeavor to consecrate his life to his Maker's service. In the hopes of again meeting beloved parents and friends in that home, which gilds the paradise above, he found that solace which could no where else be obtained, and was enabled to go on in the discharge of the duties of life, with serenity and peace.

Reader, you must soon leave your home, and leave it for ever. The privileges and the joys you are now partaking will soon pass away. And when you have gone forth into the wide world, and feel the want of a father's care, and of a mother's love, then will all the scenes you have passed through, return freshly to your mind, and the remembrance of every unkind word, or look, or thought, will give you pain. Try, then, to be an affectionate and obedient child.

Cultivate those virtues which will prepare you for usefulness and happiness in your more mature years, and above all, make it your object to prepare for that happy home above, where sickness can never enter, and sorrow can never come.

Other Related Titles from SGCB

Solid Ground Christian Books is delighted to bring back into print *buried treasure* from the past to help mold and direct the rising generation. In addition to *The Child at Home* we offer the following:

EVANGELICAL TRUTH: *Practical Sermons for the Christian Home* by Archibald Alexander (1772-1851). This volume was produced towards the end of the fruitful life of the man who was called *"the Shakespeare of the Christian heart."* This volume was published to set forth Evangelical Truth in its very essence. The author tells us that the sermons were written to be read within the family circle.

THE SCRIPTURE GUIDE: *a Familiar Introduction to the Study of the Bible* by James Waddel Alexander is the first in our series of American Sunday School Union Classic Reprints. J.W. Alexander devoted a part of his ministry for over 30 years to the Sunday School Union, writing more than 30 titles for them. Written in the form of a story, the reader is carried along on an unforgettable journey into the realm of Bible Study. Students and teachers alike will be captivated by this resource.

MY BROTHER'S KEEPER: *Letters to a Younger Brother on the Virtues and Vices, Duties and Dangers of Youth* by James W. Alexander. Buried for more than 150 years this volume contains 21 letters which are directed to young people ten years old and above. Tom Ascol, of the Founder's Movement, said, *"These letters are wonderful! Not only are they overflowing with practical wisdom for young men but they also exemplify the kind of fraternal love that ought to characterize our Lord's disciples. This is a useful tool for men who want to encourage and help younger men become faithful followers of Christ."*

LITTLE PILLOWS & MORNING BELLS by Francis Havergal. These two volumes are the perfect tool to help children begin and end each day with their minds fixed upon the Scriptures.

THE PASTOR'S DAUGHTER: *The Way of Salvation Explained to his Daughter by Rev. Edward Payson* by Louisa Payson Hopkins. Susan Hunt said, *"Grand gospel themes are woven throughout this delightful book, which is as relevant for the child as the parent."*

OLD PATHS FOR LITTLE FEET by Carol Brandt is a brand new title that is intended to help mothers and grandmothers train little ones to walk in the old paths gaining rest for our souls.

Call us toll free at **1-877-666-9469**
Visit us on the web at **solid-ground-books.com**

Printed in the United Kingdom
by Lightning Source UK Ltd.
103786UKS00001B/259-282